The
NEW ELEMENTS
of Standard
SCREENPLAY FORMAT

The
NEW ELEMENTS
of Standard
SCREENPLAY FORMAT

by Jean-Paul Ouellette

A simplified guide to the
rules and uses of standard
screenplay format in the
computer age.

Yankee Classic Pictures
Rockport, Massachusetts
www.yankeeclassic.com
editor@yankeeclassic.com

First Edition
March, 2013

Please help us in the entertainment industry prevent piracy of filmed, recorded, published, and other media. Sadly, it robs artists of the necessary income which allows us to produce our art for the public and makes it difficult for young artists to find careers in the industry.

TABLE OF CONTENTS

The
NEW ELEMENTS
of Standard
SCREENPLAY FORMAT

INTRODUCTION

A great screenplay has two functions: first, to create a world in which film viewers will become completely wrapped up in and experience an emotional response which equals or exceeds the price of the admission, and, second, to be the blueprint which can verbally project this world and its emotional content to a script reader, producer, director, actors, and crew so that they will want to make the film the screenplay describes.

The first part is the literature of screenwriting. The second is the craft.

A lot of what makes the "craft" work is the process of proper format. Script readers, producers, directors, etc., have trained themselves to read scripts, and most of this training has been on properly formatted screenplays. The format is designed to accomplish a number of things:

- It forces the screenwriter to be clear and concise.
- It makes the format disappear so the reader thinks about and sees only the story.
- It guides the filmmakers to make the film the screenwriter envisioned.
- Properly used, it creates a film which should match the script at one minute per page.
- Finally, the format should make it easy for the film crew to convert the script into useful production information.

This last point has a lot to do with the relationship between the writer and the production crew. The more the script helps them, the more the writer is considered a valuable member of the team. That is what this book is all about: keeping the screenwriter a part of the film the screenwriter created. Format is the thing which meshes the script with the actual creation of the film. A well-written screenplay should inspire the crew and actors to enhance the best qualities of the screenplay, capture the essence, and expand the visual and emotional elements. But a poorly written screenplay, even with great emotional arcs, can cause a film crew to fight against the writer, thinking that they can save the screenplay by revising it and creating a better vision.

The majority of the crew who make a motion picture do not actually read the screenplay but work from breakdowns of the script in the form of a "one-line" script (an abridged version of the script in a few pages), a breakdown book (scene by scene lists of required elements to reproduce the script), and a production schedule which lists the scenes in the order they will be shot. While this seems to separate the screenplay from much of the crew, a good screenwriter's script should be able to convert to these formats and still inspire the same dedication to the writer's original vision. The secret is that the writer's format should be able to create these production formats without losing the writer's original meaning.

A screenplay is not a novel. It is not a flowery descriptive device to show off literary prowess, unless that prowess is the ability to effectively provoke images and concepts through evocative, economical language and dialogue. It is a series of described actions and dialogue which reveals the journey of the characters through obstacles and faults which they must face and overcome to attain their goals.

Sadly, there are professionals and teachers who keep saying that screenplay format is not important. This seems a clear attempt to either "dumb-down" the profession and the craft of screenwriting or to prevent competition from young screenwriters.

All I can say is, don't be the "dumbed-down" screenwriter. Even if you are told to ignore format, don't be foolish enough to think it isn't important. You will be going up against a lot of smart writers who can and do use it. Just ask any assistant director how important screenplay format is for the production crew or a script reader at how annoying it is to read a script with bad format. Be the professional writer who is the master of the craft of screenwriting.

This guide incorporates both practical experience in Hollywood and the independent film industry and is based on the study of many original screenplay manuscripts written throughout the history of the business. The meaning and use of many elements of format have been forgotten and are refined and explained here.

It also incorporates the computer age production complexities which present new challenges to the screenwriter; complications which have not been addressed in traditional screenplay format books. Most production software was designed to work with strict format. Understanding this will help your script communicate with the assistant director and the production manager who must break down your script into the elements of production.

Grateful thanks is due to the students and faculty of the Emerson College Professional Screenwriting Certificate Program, who tested the book as it developed, especially program director Barry Brodsky and instructor Scott Anderson. Also, my special thanks to Genine Tillotson of Harvard Square Script Writers who offered substantial editing assistance.

I hope that it will be useful to others in the field of motion picture screenwriting.

The Author

CHAPTER 1
SCRIPT READERS

Script Readers, Producers, & The Audience - Assistant Directors & Production Managers - Directors, Cast, & Crews

W hile you write your screenplay to communicate to an audience, the most critical moment your script will have is when the script reader reads it. That is when the script starts its journey from words to audio-visual actuality, that is the moment that makes or breaks you. Once the script reader has finished the script and decided it is interesting, the script has survived its hardest test. And, as a writer, you must use every element of your craft and creativity to win that moment.

The people who read scripts are trained and accustomed to being given well-crafted, literate, insightful, and exciting scripts. This is accomplished by the screenwriter through a mixture of word-craft, formula, and personal creativity. The script should read smoothly, creating the images, evoking the mood, and fascinating the viewer with the emotional arc of the characters.

It is not a mechanical blueprint. If you plan on writing out every camera angle and describing every prop and actor's emotion, you're not going to get the reader interested in the project. In fact, you are more likely to bore or insult him or her. Readers expect and like a good story, not a technical manual.

SCRIPT READERS, PRODUCERS, & THE AUDIENCE

Script readers, whether studio readers, production company assistants, producers, etc., read a lot of scripts. They pick up a script and say to themselves: "Is this worth two hours of my time to read?" A script on yellow paper is hard on the eyes. A script in tiny font is hard on the eyes. A script that presents a wall of description with no breaks is hard on the eyes. A reader is likely to put down such a script and pick up the next one off the pile, if it looks more pleasant to read. Don't let this happen to your screenplay. The point of format is to assure the reader that he or she will enjoy the experience of reading. If they enjoy it, they can gauge its value to an audience. Remember, at this stage, they are the representative for the eventual audience. They are trying to put themselves into the cinema seat and see the film you've described. They also represent the producer, gauging if the script can be produced and will be worth the time, effort, and money.

A script reader usually spends two hours reading and commenting on a screenplay. If it takes longer, the reader will suspect something is wrong with the script. Ideally, it will take him or her ninety minutes to read the script, leaving them thirty minutes to write the review, a review which comments on the Premise, Plot, Characters, Theme, Dialogue, Structure, and Format of the screenplay. Your reader will attempt to summarize the story in a short synopsis, and finally suggest if the script should be a PASS, CONSIDER, or ACCEPT. Obviously, Pass is a kind word for "reject this script completely." Accept means that everything about this script is very good and the writer has done a very good job. But Consider is the tough one: it means that there is something about the script which is of value as a motion picture, but the writer is not fully up to the task, having failed in some area. Often, Consider means the writer has good ideas but is not a very good writer of screenplays and a more professional writer might improve it in a re-write. While not the worst situation, most writers would like to be "Accepted." Understanding and using Standard Screenplay Format makes it more likely the reviewer will see you as a professional and believe you should be kept with the script into production.

ASSISTANT DIRECTORS & PRODUCTION MANAGERS

The second important moment is when the Assistant Director (A.D.) or production manager breaks down the script before production. They will number the scenes, calculate the time each scene runs, break out the important elements of props, sounds, scenery, cast, special effects, etc. A.D.s appreciate good format because it makes their job easier. Many A.D.s use computer breakdown software to transform your script into a shooting script. Many of the rules found in this book will help you to make the script better prepared for this transition.

DIRECTORS, CAST, & CREW

In the end, you are talking to the director, cast, and crew of the production. Your clarity of description and format are going to be key elements in making sure they make the film you envision as the screenwriter. While you probably slaved for years to complete the perfect screenplay, they will only have a few months to prepare the production. The clearer you are, the more precise your vision, the better they will be able to understand and recreate your vision. This means they will enhance instead of rework. They will see your film in their minds and expand it with elements which will serve your story well. If they do not trust your script and feel the need to rework it to fit the needs of their production, you risk them trying to change elements which might break the careful balance you took so long to create. Some writers want to direct their own screenplay, but it's still important to write to inspire the rest of the crew and not to leave them in the dark. Give them your complete vision so that they can make it their vision: clarity is everything.

CHAPTER 2
DRAFT, SHOOTING, & FINAL SCRIPTS

Y ou have read scripts before, of course. The question is what version of the script did you read? Was it the screenwriter's version (draft script) or the version that the assistant director and the crew revised to suit the exigencies of production (the shooting script) or was it the legal concordance script (final script) which is created after the film is finished. It is important to know which version of a screenplay you are reading.

DRAFT SCRIPTS

The script written by the screenwriter is called the Draft Script. This is because the script is a draft or plan of the film. The writer's first version is often called the Rough Draft. Subsequent revisions become the First Draft (the first one ready to send out) and Second Draft, etc., until the writer, or the producer who purchases the script, is satisfied that it is ready for production.

A draft script by a writer who is writing it on his own, in the hopes that it will be purchased and made, is called a Speculative Script or Spec Script. This script will be marketed by sending it out to readers, agents, and producers who will review it. This is the script which must conform most to Standard Screenplay Format.

When a writer is hired to write a screenplay, the screenplay is called a Commissioned Script. Depending on the circumstances, this draft script may not require the precise format of a spec script since it does not have to go out into the market and compete against other scripts for the attention of producers. A writer working with a director might be told to ignore the conventions, especially when the director has a crew who is accustomed to working from a Shooting Script or just from Script Breakdowns and Production Boards.

SHOOTING SCRIPTS

The script used in production is called the Shooting Script or the Production Script. Unlike the Draft Script, the Shooting Script has each scene numbered. The crew, during production meetings, will add production notes such as camera angles, special notes about art, sound, location, wardrobe and other elements specific to the craftspeople making the film.

Because of this, this new blueprint, the Shooting Script, may be longer than the original draft script. But the length of the film, the time it should take on screen, will be based on the draft script. The Script Supervisor times the draft script with a stopwatch to ensure the film will time out correctly and these timings will be used as a guide during production, even though the shooting script might not match that timing because of annotations and expansions.

To create the shooting script, the script is locked. This anchors the page numbers so that any additions to or deletions from the script do not change the other pages. When a scene is expanded on page 12, it becomes page 12 and 12A. Page 13 does not change. The lines that are changed or added are also marked with asterisks on the right margin to indicate what is new or removed. The shooting script also has scene numbers. These are also are locked. When a scene is added it is given the scene number of the previous scene with a letter added, such as a new scene after scene 34 becomes 34A. This way scene 35 will always be scene 35. These changes are given to the crew on colored pages so that the production can easily see what has changed and that they are all on the same page (of a specific color) as they go through the production of the motion picture.

Some Shooting Scripts are so detailed that they include every shot planned for every scene with each shot numbered individually. These kinds of shooting scripts can run well over two hundred pages.

FINAL SCRIPTS

Once a film is completed, a Final Script is created. This script must match the final cut of the film. Every scene and every word of dialogue must match the film. This script is produced by a secretary, assistant editor, or staff member. It has many purposes:

- It is used to copyright the film along with an audio/visual copy of the film.
- It is used to translate the dialogue into foreign languages and as a guide for sound editors to cut the foreign language dubs into the film.
- It is the script the producers publish as the official screenplay of the film.

The Final Script does not need to follow any special rules of screenplay format since it is only a legal device and a translation guide for the foreign dubbing of the film. Depending on the transcriber, it may or may not have camera direction, scene transitions, extended description, etc. It is a record of the complete film in case later versions of the film are made in which scenes may be eliminated, shortened, or lengthened, based on various exhibitor needs such as censorship, etc. It can also be used to re-create the original version of the film should it ever be lost.

The final script can also contain time notations which indicate the start of scenes or shots. Silent film final scripts used reel numbers and shot numbers. During the sound era, some final scripts included film reel and footage numbers to indicate the start of scenes or shots or dialogue. Now, in the digital age, modern final scripts can contain SMPTE video time code numbering. These numbers assist editors inserting foreign language dialogue and titles into the film and, perhaps someday, conservation editors who may need it as reference to restore the film.

If the film company wants to exploit the film as literature, they may publish the final script for the public. This version is almost always quite removed from the original draft script that inspired the film in the first place.

CHAPTER 3
STANDARD SCREENPLAY FORMAT

Scanning - A Page Per Minute - The Evolution of the Format
- The Naysayers

H ow does Standard Screenplay Format help the writer write?
First and foremost, Standard Screenplay Format is designed
to produce a screenplay that will be filmed at approximately a page
per minute. It is also so it can be read easily in ninety minutes
(even a 120 page script). A good script is designed to be easy
on the eye. As the reader becomes interested in the story and
characters, the format should almost disappear and be replaced by
the reader's imagination of the description and dialogue.

SCANNING

Part of the ease of reading and following the rhythm of the
screenplay is the use of white space on the page. Standard
Screenplay Format and the conventions of screenwriting are
designed to allow easy "scanning." Scanning is the ability to read
across a line and down a page quickly without losing your place.
Think of how often you've lost the scan while reading a novel,
magazine, or newspaper. When this happens you momentarily
step out of what you are reading and have to find the next line
before you can begin again. In screenwriting, the goal is never
to have the reader lose his or her place or be distracted from the
experience of the story.

Toward this end, screenplay format always separates
format elements that set up a scene (scene headings) or end a
scene (transitions) by leaving a blank line before and after them
(double spacing). The elements of dialogue and description are

also separated by blank lines to make it easier to read. But scene description is single spaced, as are the dialogue blocks, and never full justified so as to leave a ragged right edge to help scanning. Dialogue blocks are indented from the left and right margins, also for ease of reading. And, as we will see later, scene description should never run more than six lines without a blank line. The subject of spacing will be discussed further with each element later.

A PAGE PER MINUTE

One of the most important things about screenplay format is that is that it produces a script which should end up being the same length in pages as the film is in minutes. This standard was developed in the silent and early sound era of films. Originally, the length of a film was limited by the physical length of reels of film. A one reel film could not have a script longer than ten to eleven minutes - the time of a one thousand foot reel of 35 millimeter film. As things like editing advanced and theaters could use two projectors, films could be longer. These early films were actually called by their number of film reels: one-reelers, three-reelers. Time was important.

Time is still important in modern films. The exhibitors, the venues which show films from theaters to television channels, set standards which help the profitability of a film. A good example is the two hour scheduling period. Cinema theaters prefer to advertise screening times that fall on the hour. This means that the film must be less than two hours: to allow people to arrive and find seats, previews to be shown, time for the audience to leave, and the theater cleaned up before the next showing. A majority of feature films are between 95 to 115 minutes long. For films longer than 115 minutes, theaters are forced to schedule irregular times. Films which are designed for high box office potential can run longer; i.e., the epic or event films, which run two hours or longer.

For television, the preference has also been the two hour movie block. Since television also requires station breaks for identification and commercials, television films are usually 80 to 90 minutes long to work in a two hour block. Many films are edited for content and for time on television since station breaks and advertising are required in the same time frame. On television a system called "drop-frame" time code can also imperceptibly speed up a film.

Before production, the script supervisor or continuity person will read the script with a stopwatch and time the script. This will be a gauge of how long each scene should last on screen and to confirm the overall length of the film. This timing will be checked during production to know if they are sticking to the timing of the screenplay or varying from it. In general, a page of solid dialogue runs about 45 seconds and a page of action will run about 75-90 seconds. Average these out and you should get just about a page per minute.

It is often good to have your script read aloud by a group of professionals (a narrator and actors) to confirm that it does run about a page per minute. When read silently, a reader will able to do it under 90 minutes.

THE EVOLUTION OF THE FORMAT

Early silent films were usually adaptations of literary works, mostly novels. But the running time of these early films were limited by the length of the reels of film they were shot on. One reel of film, about one thousand feet, would last about ten minutes. The short length of films required the writer to condense the story down. For instance, the 1902 film *From the Earth to the Moon* was a fourteen minute film adapted from Jules Verne's one hundred and fifty something page novel *De la Terre à la Lune*. The screenwriter's adaptations became known as a "treatment" of a longer work. As film conventions such as title cards and dialogue cards were added to help the audience follow the story, the treatment was adapted to include these elements. If you research early film scripts, you will see the rudimentary screenplay format emerging. Since silent films, because of their lack of spoken language, were international, they needed a final script to help with the translation of the title cards and dialogue cards with specific instructions as to where they should be inserted into the film.

As silent films developed into two-reel, three reel, and then ten-reel films and filmmakers attempted more complex plots and the production crews needed to make a film became larger, the scripts needed to become more sophisticated and address the needs of a larger and more diverse group of film craftsmen and technicians. In a studio situation, where films were being pounded out week after week, standardization was essential.

Format evolved from a collaboration between screenwriters and typists and producers. Yes, back in the olden days writers had typists; now, sadly, a practically obsolete profession. Back then, writers would hand write or type their scripts. Corrections were often handwritten notes in the margins. These were sent over to the studio typing pools where typists would re-type the work into clear and readable scripts. Since many writers had different styles, it was the typing pools who began to organize a system where each script would have a standardized look so that the producers, directors, actors, and crew going from project to project would have a standard language to work from.

Scene headings, transitions, and shape of dialogue blocks were developed and screenwriters now had a framework in which they could be creative and still communicate the technical aspects of production to a cast and crew. In this way, the writer, using proper format, can concentrate on the creative elements of story, description, and dialogue. You will often hear the word "slug" used to describe format terms. A slug is the slot on the page reserved for format while the non-slug area is the writer's creative area.

While secretaries and production assistants today are the people who write the Final Script for production companies, the burden of writing with proper Standard Screenplay Format falls to the screenwriter. Screenplay format has been in place for over a century and is well ingrained across the industry. It is a language that each screenwriter must understand, master, and follow to ensure that the words on the page become the images and words that the audience sees and hear from the finished motion picture.

THE NAYSAYERS

There has been a move in the film business to lessen the position of the screenwriter. And much of this can be blamed on bad screenwriters. Besides just writing terrible stories which no one wants to see, many screenwriters have begun to infringe on the creative decisions of the filmmakers. Failing to master format has created a lot of poor scripts which insult filmmakers by trying to do their job. This is why good screenwriters—even directors who write—avoid using camera, actor, and editing direction in a screenplay. If we don't use a style of writing that inspires creativity in the production crew, the crew—from directors and cinematographers to actors—may feel insulted that they are not being allowed to use their creative powers. They don't want to be directed by the writer, but allowed to embellish the writer's work. It can be a battle of egos. The more a screenwriter tries to be controlling, the more the screenwriter will be unappreciated and not considered part of the production team. Being a better writer is the way to avoid this conflict. Produce a well-crafted screenplay which inspires the crew to make your film and you will be part of the team.

So, when someone tells you it doesn't matter if you use proper screenplay format or not...? Don't listen to them. You are a professional writer. Would you take the advice of someone who tells you that grammar, spelling, and punctuation don't really matter and you don't have to use them properly? No, you are smarter than that.

CHAPTER 4
SCREENPLAY SOFTWARE AND
FILM PRODUCTION SOFTWARE

This guide will keep making reference to the software which can be used to write your screenplay (Screenwriting Software) and the software which filmmakers use to prepare your script for production (Production Software which includes Breakdown, Scheduling, and Budgeting).

Most screenwriting software is not automatically correct in its formatting and you must impose on it the correct screenplay format rules, the same rules you would have if you were using pen and paper, typewriter, or a word processor.

You also need to have some understanding of how your script will be broken down by a film production. This will help bridge the divide many see between screenwriters and production. Making the job of the production crew easier, makes you more of a crew member than an adversary they must battle with.

SCRIPTWRITING SOFTWARE

The professional screenwriter does not "need" a screenwriting software program. A screenplay can just as easily be written with a pen and paper, a typewriter (what's that?), or any text editing or word processing program on any type of computer. And screenplay format is actually as easy as knowing about margins and tabs and being able to use the Tab Key and be able to Left/Right Indent. You don't need special software for that. But, since it is available, it can be very useful.

Screenwriting software was not developed for screenwriters. It was developed for people who want to be screenwriters. It was designed to reach the widest possible consumer audience. So screenwriting software includes a lot of things professional screenwriters rarely use and some things a professional screenwriter would not be caught dead using. Remember, just because the software includes something, it does not mean you should use it.

But there are good reasons for using screenwriting software. Many of them do have features which are useful to the screenwriter and allow you to look at your screenplay in various ways to help see and revise substance, form, and format. Some have adjunct elements such as index story cards, smart typing, scene and location reports, and conversion to a shooting script. And if you start on a screenplay software, you can master the useful functions and ignore those you don't need.

One of the important aspects of using screenwriting software is when you are selling a screenplay. The production company will want your screenplay in a format which can mesh into production software. Authoring on one of the major screenwriting software programs makes this possible.

But the software itself isn't going to make you write a great screenplay. Screenwriting software packages do the formatting for you as you go along. Sometimes they don't have the flexibility of the major word processors like WordPerfect® (which can left/right indent properly for dialogue and search and replace formatting) and Microsoft Word® (which uses change margins for indenting dialogue) which can bullet point and handle unusual format problems But there are always work-arounds which you can find.

Software such as industry standard Final Draft® and Movie Magic Screenwriter® or the open-source Celtx all have their uses and added elements which can help organize and track your screenplay. The best software is the one that works best for you.

A screenwriter who knows how to affect the emotions of a reader might want to cheat the system to create a formatting effect. Sometimes you don't want the car crash to be on the bottom of the page but have the crash come after you turn the page. Sometimes a montage or shot series may require a bullet point list which may not be available in the software. Most format systems don't worry about things like that. A good screenwriter does.

See which software serves and suits you best.

Some of the current Screenwriting Software Programs are:

- Final Draft®
- Scrivener Writing®
- Movie Magic Screenwriter®
- Movie Outline®
- Montage®
- Celtx
- MediaWiki ScreenPlay Extension
- Plotbot Online Script Editor

For writers who prefer using word processing software such as Microsoft Word®, Corel WordPerfect®, Open Office®, etc., there are formatting templates and macro programs which can assist in quick format during typing.

FILM PRODUCTION SOFTWARE

Once a script is written and purchased, it is handed over to a production team who will work with the script to produce a number of documents which are used during the making of the motion picture.

The first process is to "break down" the script. Scene numbers are assigned to each scene header. The script is "locked" so that the draft script's page numbers will not be changed. Some software have taggers where the crew can highlight mentioned elements like props, sounds, effects, costumes, etc., so that they automatically transfer to the breakdown software, making it unnecessary for the screenwriter to capitalize sound or props in the script. Then it is usually parsed into a breakdown software. This software reads the script into a database which automatically separates the scene numbers, setting, location and set, time of day, and individual characters speaking in a scene. It also measures each scene in increments of one-eighth of a page. This will become the blueprint that the crew uses to manufacture the film. This database creates a breakdown page for each scene which allows the crew to enter additional elements which are needed to make the scene come to life. Before production starts, each breakdown page will list everything which will be needed for a scene from actors to camera and lighting equipment, extras, set dressing and props, special effects equipment, sound considerations, etc. It also has a short description of the scene. The breakdown is far more detailed than a screenplay can be. It will be used as the central source of all production information. From the breakdown database, the production generates most of the paperwork and information they need to make the motion picture.

Once the breakdown is completed, the assistant director will arrange the scene information on a production strip board. The strips allow the A.D. to shuffle the scenes to create a schedule of the most logical order in which to film the scenes. The main considerations will be what and when actors and locations are needed and available. From the breakdown and the schedule, a budget can be made based on the time it will take to film each location with the actors, crew and equipment needed.

For most of the crew, the breakdown pages, put together as a book they carry, will be their most important tool, more important than the original script. This book may also contain set and location plans, storyboards, shooting plots, etc. The breakdown also can produce a list of scenes and their short description (called a one-line script) and daily call sheets with lists of everyone and everything needed on a specific day.

If your script does not easily translate into the breakdown, the assistant director and others will have to do a lot of additional work, which they will curse the writer for. So, the better your format, the more you will be appreciated by the crew making your story into a film.

CHAPTER 5
THE BLACK TYPE

Font - Monospacing Type - Courier Fonts - Sentence Spacing

T he appearance of your script is important. The readers of your script are going to want it to be easy to read. This adds to its ability to create the visual and aural imagery you want to bring the reader into your story.

FONT

The type should be clear and dark against the white page, and very legible. The standard type face for a screenplay is typewriter Courier. This is Courier Monotype or Courier PICA. It is the easiest on the eye. It is the right size for proper formatting, and it is the only one you should use. Monotype fonts, also called fixed-pitch, fixed-width or non-proportional, or non-kerning fonts, keep the spacing between letters identical, making the characters per line consistent and easier to read.

Why? The reason for using a standardized, non-kerning font is so that every script has the same number of character spaces per line. This is important for both action and dialogue.

MONOSPACING TYPE

Look at the difference in these dialogue lines below.

```
            MONOTYPE COURIER
iiiiiiiii aaaaaaaaa eeeeeeeee 32
mmmmmmmmm ttttttttt sssssssss 32
```

You will notice that every letter is the same width. This means that there is a standard or set number of characters per line.

In this example 32. But other fonts which kern—vary the space between letters—produce variable numbers of characters per line as shown here.

KERNING ARIAL

iiiiiiiii iiiiiiiii iiiiiiiii iiiiiiiii iiiiiiiii iiiiiiiii iiiiiiiii iiiiiiiii 82
mmmmmmmmmm mmmmmmmmmm mmm 26

It is important in the timing of a screenplay that the number of character is the same on each line. This is especially true for dialogue.

COURIER FONTS

There are a number of monotype typefaces on the market for screenwriters which imitate the old typewriter fonts and most screenwriting software comes with a monotype font built in. Monospacing fonts can be found and purchased on the net or through screenwriter's groups or advertised in screenwriter's magazines. These allow you to adhere to the standard while enjoying the advantages of a computer. They also have the look and immediacy of hand-typed scripts.

The most accepted screenplay typeface is Courier, a monospacing font. Many recommend Courier 10 BT.

```
The quick brown fox jumped over
the lazy dog's back.
```

Most screenwriting software comes with a variation of Courier. This version of Courier comes with Final Draft® software.

```
The quick brown fox jumped over
the lazy dog's back.
```

SENTENCE SPACING

The big question for screenwriters is whether to use one or two spaces between sentences. Currently, the convention is to use one space after a period and before the next sentence (called "French Spacing"). This has become common in the computer age where kerning squeezes letters closer and a single space seems larger. But when the typewriter was invented, it could only use monospacing type and to make reading easier two spaces were used between sentences ("English Spacing").

The typewriter was invented in 1866. The personal computer replaced it in the 1980s with the release of the low cost (about the same as a car) PC computers and word processing machines. When motion pictures were invented the typewriter was the screenwriters tool of choice. Because of this the monospacing convention remains the standard for screenplays today.

So the question for screenwriters is:

To make your screenplay more readable, for the scan of the line and the ease of the eye, do you double space after a period and before the next sentence or do you use only one space?

```
This is the "English Spacing" where two
spaces follow the period.  It is up to the
writer if this is better on the eye.  While
the tradition has been two spaces, it is
still a matter of preference.
```

```
This is the "French Spacing." Only
one space is used. And it may not seem
different from the two space version.
```

So type a few pages of your script. Read it through thinking about how it reads across the page. Which is easier to look at, to read, to see the picture you are describing and stick with that choice. Two spaces is traditional, one space is contemporary. Either is currently acceptable.

CHAPTER 6
MARGINS AND TABS

Margins - Tab Stops - Formatting Keys

Y ou don't need screenwriting software to write. But you need to set up the page for the screenplay format. Ideally every screenplay should be formatted the same. For instance, the margins on the page make the typing area 6.4 inches wide and 9 inches high. Each page is 54 lines long. Using monospacing fonts, a line is 55 characters long while a line of dialogue is 35 characters long. This should mean that every screenwriter, regardless of his or her style of writing, will be working with the same page formula, and that, in the 90-120 pages the script will run, the pages will average one page per minute.

The following are the page measurement rules which fulfill the Standard Screenplay Format.

MARGINS

Make your margins:

LEFT MARGIN=1.75" and RIGHT MARGIN=.1.0"
TOP MARGIN-1.0" and BOTTOM MARGIN=1.0"

A note about margins. Some writers who have an overlong screenplay sometimes attempt to cheat the margins to make their script seem shorter. Don't! Most readers know this trick. And it will appear unprofessional.

The 1.75" left margin takes into account the three-hole punched page and the eventual scene numbering which is added at 1.25" from left edge of the page.

TAB STOPS

You are going to need only four tab stops (measured from the left edge of the page). Your Scene Headers and Description start on the left margin but everything else falls on a Tab.

FIRST TAB STOP=2.75" for start of dialogue
SECOND TAB STOP=3.5" for start of parentheticals
    (personal direction)
THIRD TAB STOP=3.75" for start of character cue
FOURTH TAB STOP=6.25" for both start of a scene
    transition and end of dialogue. Note: Some
    software use right justify for scene transitions.

FORMATTING KEYS

If you are not using screenwriting software but working in a standard word processor, there should be only two formatting keys you need to use.

For Character Cues, Parentheticals, and Scene Transitions, you use the TAB key. If the Transition laps over to the next line you can Right Justify the line to the right margin.

For Dialogue, you use the LEFT/RIGHT INDENT key (which may be is a combination of keys) or LEFT/RIGHT MARGIN INDENT (usually a macro shortcut you create).

For most word processors there are macro packages for screenwriters which have prepared shortcuts for all the format elements. These can be found on the internet and are either free or available for a reasonable price.

CHAPTER 7
PAGE NUMBERS

Page Numbers - Headers and Footer - Page Continued

T he page numbers are always justified to the upper right hand corner of the page one inch down and three quarters of an inch from the right edge of the page. You can, if you want, format it with or without a period after the page number.

The page number line should contain no other writing and have a blank line below it. Do not put the name of your script at the top of each page, this is just annoying to the reader.

The opening page (page 1) usually does not have a number since it might have the title across the top. Screenwriting software does this automatically. If you are using Microsoft Word or Corel WordPerfect, you need to set a page number delay to create this effect

Example. (Numbered page 12)

12

Mary moved around the bush to the bench.
On it she found the missing knife.

HEADERS AND FOOTERS

If you are working on a word processing software other than one designed for screenwriting, the only header you should use is one for numbering the pages. Do not have headers or footers which give any other information. Do not put the name of the script or your name or any other information on the page.

Anything extraneous which repeats over and over again in a script becomes annoying to a reader who is trying to read your script carefully.

PAGE "CONTINUED"

"CONTINUED" at the bottom and top of pages to indicate that a scene continues is another annoyance. It is a convention left over from the days of live radio scripts. They were for performers who have to look forward to see if the scene ends at the bottom of a page or goes on to the next. If it went on, they had to turn their pages quietly, so the home audience would not hear, and continue speaking.

In film production, it is sometimes used in shooting scripts when revised pages are handed out. It means that the original page has been expanded onto an additional page and the continued slug may also include a number to show just how many pages have been added.

Readers know that if there is not a scene transition at the bottom of the page the scene generally continues to the next page. Screenplays do not allow a transition to start a new page. Transitions are block protected to the action or dialogue that comes before it, preventing it from becoming a widow on the next page. This will be covered in more depth in the Transitions chapter.

CHAPTER 8
OPENINGS & ENDINGS

Fade In and Fade Out - The End - Credits

T he first element on the first page is a repeat of the title. This is in case the cover is torn off. The first page does not have a page number because of this. The title may be all capitals and underlined and centered but should be no larger than the standard 12 point type of the rest of the screenplay. If you're using Screenwriting software, make sure the title doesn't register as a scene header but as general text or action.

Example. (First page, no page number, and the title centered)

                    MURDER IN THE MANSION

                                        FADE IN:

EXT. SCOTTISH MOORS - NIGHT

MARY, the beautiful daughter of the Thane,
dressed in a flowing light blue robe,
wanders barefoot across the moonlit moor.

"FADE IN:" is the traditional opening of a script and is the only time that is used in a script. We recommend you use the colon and make it a scene transition so it is not mistaken as a Scene Header, which would mean it might get a scene number and throw the numbering off. The convention is that this is the moment after the audience has gotten used to the blackened theater, the movie begins - its light coming up and filling the screen and the imagination of the audience.

"FADE OUT" is the traditional last words of a screenplay. You can also use "THE END." "FADE OUT:" is inserted as a transition while "THE END" is usually centered and can be underlined on the final page.

Example. (End page)

```
Morris and Mary clutch each other and kiss.
Beyond them, the water boils up, spouting
steam.  The Monster thrashes one last time
to the surface before sinking slowly to the
bottom.

                              FADE OUT:
```

It is also acceptable to use The End centered after the last of the script instead:

```
              THE END
```

CREDITS

Generally, screenwriters do not include instructions for titles or credits in a screenplay unless they are so integral to the storytelling and feel of the opening or ending that they must be included. This is pretty rare. If, for some reason, you have an opening sequence involving title and credits, write it simply accenting the visuals and not the titles. Generally, motion pictures without elaborate animated or graphical title sequences like to unobtrusively insert titles and credits under the opening scene of the story, usually as it reveals the geography of the setting or to complete the titles in as graphics before the story begins.

CHAPTER 9
SCENE HEADINGS

Setting - Location, Set - Additional Heading Elements - Time
of Day - For Professionals Only - Period, Comma, and Hyphen
- Continuous and Same Time - Moments Later and Next Day -
Angle On and Another Angle - Back to Scene - Scene Numbers

E ach time the story moves to a new scene, in space or time,
the new setting is established with a Scene Heading, also
called a Scene Header or Scene Slug. It should appear on one line
and not wrap to a second line. This is a traditional formula of three
elements and starts at the left margin.

Used properly, the Scene Heading is unobtrusive and the
reader will, as the script goes on, breeze over it and concentrate on
the story instead of the format.

The most powerful use of the Scene Heading is to include:
SETTING. LOCATION, SET - TIME OF DAY. This assures
both clarity of reading and that this heading will be useful in the
production of the motion picture adaptation of the script. The use
of computers in modern production has required the screenwriter
to be very accurate in scene headings.

Example: (Four sample scene headings.)

```
INT. SUMMER HOUSE, TIM'S BEDROOM - NIGHT

EXT. LA AIRPORT, CUSTOMS GATE - DAY

INT/EXT. DESERT HIGHWAY, JAKE'S SEMI - DAY

EXT. LA AIRPORT (1979), (MONTAGE) - DAY
```

SETTING

The first element is the Setting (or Scene Intro). This always begins a scene heading as three capital letters followed by a period and a space. There are three choices for this.

INT, meaning Interior, is a space which is indoors, an enclosed space. A room with windows which see out on the world is still an interior since most of the lighting is either artificial light or reflected sunlight.

EXT, meaning Exterior, is any area which is outdoors or directly exposed to sky and natural light.

INT/EXT, meaning Interior And Exterior, is a setting which is primarily outdoors but has set elements which might be considered interior. It means that the characters and/or the camera will be both inside and outside during the scene. Some writers used to use I/E but it is not recognized by some production software.

INT/EXT means that the camera and actors will be outside and inside in the same scene. The most familiar example of this is a scene with a car, bus, or truck when characters are entering or exiting the vehicle. If the car were in a garage it would be an Interior. If the scene is only two people driving and the camera and characters are sitting in the car it is an Interior. But once the characters or the camera go in or out of the car in the scene it becomes an Interior/Exterior. An unusual example might be an open living room which extends into the back yard where the actors walk in and out from interior lighting to natural sunlight without separation between the two sets. The moment you separate the two sets (Interior and Exterior) into individual scenes you drop the INT/EXT designation.

LOCATION, SET

Location and Set information work together to describe the place where the scene takes place. The Location is the overall description of the place where the scene is set and the Set is a specific place within the Location. For instance, the Location might be a house or office building or national park. Once you are there, the Location is divided into Sets: house (kitchen, living room, dining room, basement, etc.); office building (lobby, elevator, reception, private office, hall, etc.); and national park (forest, mountain road, camping area, camp site, lodge, etc.) Clearly identifying your location and set allows the reader and the production company to easily know where they are in the story.

LOCATION: After the Setting, which always has a period and a space after it, comes the second element: the Location. This is a quick and descriptive title for the location. It should very briefly describe place where the scene is located, and, if needed, tell us the owner or character associated with the place. A BEDROOM is not a good location because it does not tell us where we are in a large sense. Whose bedroom, like AMY MARTIN'S BEDROOM, still doesn't tell us enough. The location in this case is going to be where the bedroom is. This bedroom is in the house owned by the Martins. The location should be the MARTIN HOUSE.

SET: Each of the components that make up a Location is called a Set. So the bedroom belonging to Amy is a set in the MARTIN HOUSE location. And it is not just a bedroom, since there are probably more than one bedroom in the house, so it is specifically AMY'S BEDROOM.

INT. MARTIN HOUSE, AMY'S BEDROOM - NIGHT

When you have an Int/Ext situation, don't call the location CAR or TRUCK CAB. These are very vague. The car is a set and you need to tell us where it is. If it's in the desert or on a city street is very important to the reader. So the car is INT/EXT. CANYON ROAD, TOM'S CAR - DAY

Using both Location and Set adds great clarity to the reading and understanding of your script. With modern production software, you are going to write the Location followed by a comma and space and the Set. The comma is used because production software does not use commas to parse information and will keep Location and Set together.

Many writers feel this is too hard to do (boy, that sounds pretty lame on the part of someone who claims to be a screenwriter) but the word processing macro and the smart typing features in most screenplay software makes it very easy.

Look at these two lists from the same script:

```
GUEST BEDROOM
JOHN' BATHROOM
KITCHEN
MARY'S GARAGE
CAR
```

or

```
DESERT HIGHWAY, TOM'S CAR
JOHN'S CONDO, BATHROOM
JOHN'S CONDO, GUEST BEDROOM
MARY'S HOUSE, GARAGE
MARY'S HOUSE, KITCHEN
```

It is pretty obvious which is clearer. By using both Location and Set in your scene headings, you make it easy to see how many sets are in each location you have created. You should always opt for the clearest format. If your script doesn't, the production company will have to go into your script and start reworking it.

ADDITIONAL HEADING ELEMENTS

If you need to use a unique scene description such as flashback, flash forward, dream sequence, establishing shot, montage, and series of shots, they can be included in Scene Headings. While non-linear and unique scenes are explained further in the chapter on scene description, they are sometimes noted in the Scene Heading. Since they are not actually sets they are differentiated by brackets ().

The flashback, dream, establishing shots (and often stock footage) are usually a specific scene with a single location and a specific time of day. They appear as part of the Location, Set:

```
EXT. MADISON HOUSE, (FLASHBACK) - DAY
INT. BLACK LIMBO, (DREAM SEQUENCE) - NIGHT
EXT. POLICE HQ, (ESTABLISHING SHOT) - DAY
INT. CONVENTION, (STOCK FOOTAGE) - NIGHT
```

For the montage or shot series, it can be more complex and needs some thought. Here are some examples.

```
EXT. MINNESOTA FARM, (MONTAGE) - DAY
INT/EXT. DOJO, (SCENE SERIES) - NIGHT
INT. NEWSPAPER OFFICES, (SHOT SERIES) -
EXT. TRANSYLVANIA MOUNTAINS (MONTAGE) -
```

Even though these may vary widely in content, you still want to attempt to adhere to the formula of the Scene Heading, if possible. When possible use INT or EXT if they are all interior or exterior. If they vary, use INT/EXT.

If they are day or night, use DAY or NIGHT. If they vary, do not include a Time of Day but put the time of day on each element in description. This will signal the A.D. to check within the scene for time of day. There will be more on this in the chapter on Description.

TIME OF DAY

Lastly, after a space-hyphen-space " - ", comes the final element: the Time of Day. There are two choices for Time of Day: "DAY" and "NIGHT." If the time of day is lit by sunlight it is DAY. If the sun is down, it is NIGHT. There should only be Day or Night at the end of the scene heading. Do not use Continuous or Later or Next Day or any term other than Day or Night.

When the script is broken down, the only important element of the Time of Day is whether it is lit as day or night. The assistant director uses specific colors for these differentiations:

INT. - DAY = White   INT. - NIGHT = Blue
EXT. - DAY = Yellow   EXT. - NIGHT = Green

If you want to indicate midnight, mid-morning, late morning, noon, afternoon, late afternoon, dinner time, early evening, etc., put it in description. Also, if the exact time is needed, such as 6:45 AM or ten o'clock in the evening, these belong in description. It's more effective to set the scene with: "Tom looks at the clock, it's 9:30 AM," "The afternoon sun glares through the windshield," or "It's midnight and the full moon shines brightly across the plain."

FOR PROFESSIONALS ONLY

Okay, most screenwriters don't understand this but there are two more Time of Day designations. But they can only be used by screenwriters who fully understand them. These are the beginning and closing moments of DAY called "MORNING" and "EVENING." These are not the morning and evening of a clock but the specific filmic lighting moments of DAY when the sun it not fully over the horizon. I add this section with great caution, since if you use these terms incorrectly, the reader and the assistant director will curse you.

When an assistant director schedules a shoot, there are two short moments of the day when the lighting is so specific that they must be scheduled differently from the normal night and day. Technically, these are a periods of daytime called dawn, twilight, sunrise, sunset, and dusk. Because the sun is not at full intensity it appears to cast a yellow or golden light. This is called, in film terms, Magic Hour or Golden Hour. While it is called an hour, it actually lasts less than that. For a screenwriter, this is a beautiful time of day. For a film crew, it is an expensive and difficult thing to film. Screenwriters should not overuse it. For instance, most of us rarely see this time of day since we are often inside either asleep or having dinner. But it can add much to a story if used rarely and properly.

When breaking down the script, the assistant director will decide that a scene should be scheduled for this lighting. Usually they will cue off of the description, like "The farmer steps out of the farmhouse as the sun breaks the horizon." The assistant director will mark this time of day as "morning" in the breakdown and give it a color different from Day (a color such as salmon or orange). While interior sets and some exterior locations can be artificially lit to recreate Magic Hour, if the sky or the rising (or setting) sun is seen, it must be scheduled exactly.

If you need the scene (for dramatic purposes) to take place as the sun is about to come up (dawn), just brightening the sky (twilight) or appearing and rising on the horizon (sunrise, sun-up) you can use the term MORNING as the Time of Day. If the sun is disappearing on the horizon (sunset), just below the horizon (twilight), or just about to go to darkness (dusk), you use the Time of Day EVENING.

If you use these terms, you must also further define them in the opening description for that scene. Doing this proves you have a reason and are not just being "artsy."

PERIOD, COMMA, AND HYPHEN

It is important that you use the same spacing and punctuation for every Scene Headings. The traditional format is:

```
INT. LOCATION, SET - DAY
```

SETTING(period)(space)LOCATION(comma)(space) SET(space)(hyphen)(space)TIME

Scene Headings have only one period, after the Setting, and one hyphen, before the Time of Day.

The heading should not wrap and, ideally, not go completely across the page. The shorter the better. Some production software will cut off the end of the line if it is too long. Leave out unneeded words. Better to use SMITH HOUSE instead of THE SMITH'S HOUSE. Again, you are working with the production to make your film, not against them.

WHY? When the script is someday "parsed" by a computer into a production schedule software, the computer "reads" the Scene Heading. It expects that the first letters are going to be the Setting followed by a period and a space. What follows the period and space is the Location and Set. The Location and Set are separated by a comma which the computer knows to ignore and keeps these two items together. It then looks for a space hyphen space and reads what follows it as the Time of Day. If you do not follow this accurately, the computer cannot read the Scene Heading properly. But if you do it properly, not only is it easier to read, but the filmmakers who break down your script will have well organized and accurate scene and location reports and the script will move easily into production software.

CONTINUOUS and SAME TIME

These are often offered by screenwriting software as components of the Scene Heading. We suggest you never use these. They are actually dealt with through Scene Transitions.

There is no time of day called CONTINUOUS. It is a meaningless word, considering that the job of a screenwriter is clarity. It should mean that this scene is directly continuous with the previous scene, like someone carrying the turkey from the kitchen directly into the dining room. That is continuous. But, if you use this instead of an actual Time of Day, the production team will need to rework your screenplay with correct time of day. Unclear terms like CONTINUOUS make it hard during the non-linear scheduling of production to figure out what time of day the scene is to be shot in. If you use this word, production software will reject it as not a Time of Day and leave it blank. If you do this, you are giving the production permission to rewrite your script because you are not doing the job right.

All scenes are continuous if you don't use a transition, the No Transition option. It's as simple as that. This will be explained in the Transitions chapter.

SAME TIME, or more quizzically SAME, has the same problem. What actually does it mean? That this scene happens at the same time as the last one and you probably should split the screen to show both running simultaneously? It is an imprecise term and meaningless to most readers and filmmakers. Again, it's much more descriptive to write as opening description: "At the same time Tom drives to Vegas, Tina ..." It's kind of like the old line: "Meanwhile, back at the ranch..."

LATER and NEXT DAY

There are two phrases which some screenwriters employ in scene headings: "NEXT DAY" and "LATER." Sometimes they are used alone in a scene as if it were a Scene Heading. These are scene description and more effectively used there.

```
INT. TOM'S HOUSE, KITCHEN - DAY

The next day, Tom tries to make chocolate
chip pancakes.
```

If you feel the need to use them, embed them in Location, Set. You should indicate that it is not Location or Set by putting it in parentheses. This way it will not interfere with the logic of the scene heading.

```
INT. TOM'S HOUSE, KITCHEN (NEXT DAY) - DAY
```

Don't use time notations as scene headings or shortcuts to avoid having to write a scene heading. Here is an example of how not to use a moment later.

```
INT. THE CAFE MOROCCO, BAR - NIGHT

James pays for his brandy and sips it as
the Barman moves to other guests.

A MOMENT LATER

As James signals to the Barman for another,
Jenny comes into the barroom and slips up
behind James.
```

In this case "A MOMENT LATER" may fail to explain what is different from what went before and why we jumped forward in time. This is actually a change of scene - not a change in location or set. It is a jump forward in time and should be a full scene heading. You should write it like this.

```
INT. THE CAFE MOROCCO, BAR - NIGHT

James pays for his brandy and sips it as
the Barman moves to other guests.

INT. THE CAFE MOROCCO, BAR - NIGHT

Later, as James signals to the Barman
for another brandy, Jenny comes into the
barroom and slips up behind James.
```

In this case, the story jumps a few minutes later when James has finished his brandy, showing he's had to wait a while for Jenny to arrive. We didn't need to watch him drink the whole drink, and because we didn't move to a new location or set, there was no need for a Cut To. But we needed to put a scene heading in to indicate the change in time.

If you want to jump to another location and set and call it a Moment Later, you still need a Cut To and insert a full heading for the new location. Often the fact that it is a moment later is obvious to the reader and the audience and your noting it will only seem redundant.

ANGLE ON and ANOTHER ANGLE

While these are often dropped into scenes as description, they are actually camera direction and should be avoided. They will be better dealt with in the chapter of action description.

They are mentioned here since they often are mistaken for scene headings because they are capitalized as shown below.

ANOTHER ANGLE

Many screenwriting programs assume that any line starting with a series of capitalized words must be a scene heading. If you work in non-screenwriting software, it is likely when someone opens the file in their screenwriting software, that software will automatically change the designation of the line with all capitals to a Scene Heading. This can be confusing along the way to production.

BACK TO SCENE

Many screenwriters try to use BACK TO SCENE as a way to indicate that a closeup was shown and you are supposed to pull back to see the whole scene. This is obviously a filmmaking direction. It really serves no purpose. Again, in most screenwriting software, any line which is upper case is considered a Scene Heading and deserves a new scene number. That would incorrectly add a scene to the script the writer didn't mean to have there. Readers also look at this as a new scene heading (albeit an amateur writer's one). So it is a meaningless term and should never be used in a screenplay.

If you see this term in a screenplay it is more likely a shooting or final script. In those cases it is sometimes used as a scene heading if a shot is going to be done by a second film unit and it will get a scene sub number or as an indicator that a close up contains something that needs to be translated in foreign versions.

SCENE NUMBERS

Scene numbers are only used in the production version of a screenplay (the shooting script). Production companies don't even use scene numbered scripts when they send out a reading versions of a screenplay to attract actors or crew for the film. Scene numbers in a script, while important during production, make it less pleasant to read.

The only time a writer might use scene numbers (and only if you are using screenwriting software) is as a quick check to see if the software is mistaking non-scene heading as scene headings or to see how many scenes you have in your script. As you grow as a screenwriter, you will be able to tell if there are too many scenes in your script for the desired or expected budget. Too many scenes often makes it more difficult or expensive to film, since each scene takes time to set up and shoot. On the other hand, as you improve as a writer, you will be better at cutting between scenes, a writing style which creates more scene numbers but still keeps the script from having too many locations and sets. This may sound confusing but keep writing and you will understand this as you master the format.

Once you look at your script with scene numbers, turn them off and keep writing. Don't ever send your draft script out with scene numbers!

CHAPTER 10
SCENE TRANSITIONS

Transitions as Screenwriting Language - Cut To: - No Transition - Dissolve To: - Intercut With: - Transitions You Shouldn't Use

S ome writers don't worry about Scene Transitions (also called scene breaks). They just write on. But the Scene Transition was created for screenwriters, not filmmakers. It is a means for the screenwriter to reset the reader in time and place. A Scene Transition also gauges the time to end a scene or set up the next one. This is why it is important to standard screenplay format.

Each scene ends with a Scene Transition, unless there is a reason not to. This is usually a simple "CUT TO:" and a blank line. The four most common scene transitions are "CUT TO" and "DISSOLVE TO:" and "INTERCUT WITH:" and No Transition, which is not putting in a transition to indicate the scene is continuous into the next scene.

TRANSITIONS AS SCREENWRITING LANGUAGE

There are some who think that adding transitions is imposing camera or editing direction into a screenplay. Actually transitions are not camera direction or editing terms at all. They are specific to the screenwriter's language.

Using a scene transition does not necessarily mean the film will have that specific filmic transition, but the reader will understand how the story is moving along and where we are going.

WHY? There are a number of reasons to use transitions correctly. The most important is that in Standard Screenplay Format, the scene transition is the time it will take for the audience to react to the new scene. Each time the audience is brought into a new scene, there is a momentary adjustment, a pause needed to re-orient themselves to the change in setting, location, set, or time. The fraction of space which the scene transition takes in the script page is that moment. Directors and cinematographers will want this time to set a scene.

The four screenwriter's scene transitions are:

CUT TO:
DISSOLVE TO:
INTERCUT WITH:
No Transition to indicate a continuous scene

Note that all transitions are locked (block protected) to the description or dialogue before it. They never appear alone at the top of the next page.

Cheating by leaving out transitions can cause an average of about three to four minute discrepancy between the length of your script and the final film. Readers, producers, and studio executives are wise to this cheat. Leaving out transitions is a problem you might have to face in the long run. Learn to use them properly.

CUT TO:

CUT TO: is the most common transition. Most stories are told in linear time - the way life is lived. It indicates that the next scene is a move forward in linear time or space. The next scene is a natural progression in linear time, either a moment later or a long time later. It also is used to signify the end of a shot series, a montage, or intercut scenes.

Example 1. (Scene ends and the location cuts to another location.)

and dug the knife out of the beach sand.

                              CUT TO:

EXT. THE OLD MANSION, FRONT LAWN - NIGHT

The reason for this transition is to indicate to the reader of the change and to leave screen time for the filmmakers to establish the next scene. How often have you seen a film cut to a police detective squad room and the scene opened with a long dolly or pan across cops bringing in prisoners and the hustle and bustle of the place before the camera came to rest on the main character and the scene actually began? This is common in the film production of a script. The director and cinematographer have the time the CUT TO reserves for them to establish the transition and direct the audience's attention to the center of the scene.

The screenwriter uses the words CUT TO for a reason unrelated to the production's final editorial transition. All transitions forward in time or space for the screenwriter are the same CUT TO and no other term is used.

CUT TO is also used to end a non-linear scene (flashback, imaginary scene, etc.) to signal the return to linear time or to end of a series of scenes or shots which did not have transitions. The Cut To is the screenwriter's definitive end to a scene, series or sequence.

DISSOLVE TO:

Dissolve To is used to transition into all scenes which are not linear to the main story. It means that the next scene is not a logical move forward in time or space but a transition into a different time or space. This might be a dream scene, a flashback, a memory of something which might be real or imagined, a story told by a character which might be real or imaginary, or even a flash forward. It tells the reader that what comes next is not linear.

It is not an editing term and does not say to use a dissolve cut. It is just a means for the screenwriter to indicate that the next scene is a departure from a linear timeline.

While Dissolve To is used to enter the non-linear scene, the non-linear scene is ended with a Cut To which returns the reader to the linear story.

```
INT. TOM APARTMENT, LIVING ROOM - NIGHT

                    SARAH
        You don't remember, do you?

Tom looks out the window.

                              DISSOLVE TO:

INT. LAS VEGAS, WEDDING CHAPEL - DAY

Tom, sweating profusely, holds Sarah's
hand.

                    TOM
        I Do.

                                   CUT TO:

INT. TOM'S APARTMENT, LIVING ROOM - DAY

Tom nods at Sarah and wipes the sweat from
his brow.
```

INTERCUT WITH:

Intercut With is sometimes used when there are two scenes which are simultaneous and are inter-related. For instance, a phone conversation or a control room and the live action it is observing. If you were to cut back and forth with constant scene headings, the page count would be much longer than the time it would actually take to put the scenes on screen.

Intercut allows you to combine the scenes, staying on the more interesting one until you need to indicate some specific action on the other side (the other scene) of the action. It helps adjust length of the script to match the proper timing of the action and it tells the filmmakers to shoot both scenes in their entirety and that the editor can choose how to cut back and forth in post-production.

Example of the basic Intercut With:

```
INT. FITZ HOUSE, JOHN'S DEN - NIGHT

John picks up the phone and dials.

                    JOHN
          Joan?  Yes, I've got the answer
          to your question.

                              INTERCUT WITH:

INT. FLOWER SHOP, COUNTER - NIGHT

Joan waves to a departing CUSTOMER.

                    JOAN
          So, is it the roses or the
          lilies?

                    JOHN
          The roses.
```

```
                    JOAN
         So, when do you want them
         delivered?

                                    CUT TO:

INT. FITZ HOUSE, JOHN'S DEN - NIGHT

                    JOHN
         Wednesday morning will be fine.

John hangs up the phone.
```

In this example, the period of time in the flower shop covers the majority of the conversation. John's dialogue doesn't have a (FILTERED) Vocal Origination. When the script is broken down, John will appear in the Flower Shop scene even though he is not physically there. The assistant director breaking down the script will know that Intercut With means that the Flower Shop scene and the scene in John's Den will be shot in their entirety and that the editor can cut back and forth between them as seems logical. The Intercut With used as a transition is more visible to the A.D. than if it were buried in description and it means that the correct second scene heading is already in the script.

During the intercut, the screenwriter has decided that seeing John is not important since he has no specific action. But the A.D. will plan to shoot all John's phone conversation heard in the Flower Shop when they shoot the John's Den scene. In editing, should the editor decide some of the conversation will be heard over the phone, it will be filtered then.

Choose which is the more important side of the conversation, the one where the action is important. You cannot describe what's going on in the first scene while in the other scene. If it is important you can Intercut With back to the other scene with a scene heading to describe action there.

The Intercut With always ends with the next Cut To transition.

NO TRANSITION

This is the complement of the CUT TO. There are a number of situations where you will want to drop the CUT TO transition. When there is no time or space to the successive scene you drop the transition to reduce the space between the scenes.

First of these is the CONTINUOUS or connected scenes. If a character walks from the living room to the kitchen you can drop the "CUT TO:" since the scene are so interconnected that a camera might follow a character from one scene to the next. Not using a CUT TO indicates a continuous scene. Even if the director and cinematographer ultimately decide not to link the two scenes with a continuous shot, it still could have been done that way. The screenwriter's dropping of the Cut To indicates the closeness of the two scenes.

Example. (Scene ends and the location cuts to an adjoining location. Note how the second scene does not use CONTINUOUS as the Time of Day.)

```
INT. FITZ HOUSE, KITCHEN - NIGHT

Amy puts on her oven mitts, lifts the huge
plate of steaming turkey, and heads out.

INT. FITZ HOUSE, DINING ROOM - NIGHT

Amy enters with the turkey and places it in
front of her father.
```

The second use of the No Transition is scenes which intercut back and forth between inter-related scenes (called cross-cutting or parallel action). This usually means that the two or more scenes are happening at the SAME TIME. Once you establish each of the scenes and begin to cut between them, you can drop the Cut To. The audience does not need constant reintroduction so repeated Cut To's make the sequence overlong by page count. A Cut To stops the cross-cut sequence.

EXT. IRAQ VALLEY, OVERLOOK - NIGHT

The American SEAL Team, led by MAJOR TARR,
slips up to the overlook above the camp.
The Major signals the RADIO MAN.

                    RADIO MAN
          We're in place, sir.

                                        CUT TO:

INT. SEAL HQ, OPERATIONS CENTER - NIGHT

General Simms leans to the microphone.

                    SIMMS
          Roger. Operation is go.

EXT. IRAQ VALLEY, OVERLOOK - NIGHT

Major Tarr signals the men to move forward.

INT. SEAL HQ, OPERATIONS CENTER - NIGHT

On the General's screen a thermal view
shows Tarr's Seal team move into the camp.

EXT. IRAQ VALLEY, TERRORIST CAMP - NIGHT

Tarr and his men slip up behind three
guards and silently knock them out.

The third use of the No Transition is in a Scene Series,
where fast cut scenes create the illusion of a montage. If you need
to show a quick series of scene in rapid succession, you can drop
the Cut To to show the speed needed to make the sequence work.

INT. WHITE HOUSE, OVAL OFFICE - DAY

                    PRESIDENT WILLIAMS
          Do we know who's it is?

The President picks up the phone.

INT. RUSSIAN PALACE, BEDROOM - NIGHT

The Premier's phone rings. He groans and answers.

                    PREMIER
          Nyet, it's not our missile.
          I'll conference in the Chairman.

EXT. BEIJING, TIANANMEN SQUARE - DAY

An Official with a cell phone runs to the Chairman, who is doing Tai Chi with a group of bodyguards.

                    CHAIRMAN
          I don't care who sent it up!
          We're also ready for a fight!

INT. WHITE HOUSE, OVAL OFFICE - DAY

The President leans back in his chair.

                    PRESIDENT
          Let's take a time out here.

As above, a series of scenes is a progression of quick scenes. Each successive scene is logically related to the last, making it unnecessary to spend scene set-up time since each will flow in the next in the audience's mind. Each scene is introduced with a scene heading and gives the description and dialogue needed. By dropping the CUT TO: between the scenes, it gives the impression of a montage and the page timing will match its natural film timing.

When a pair or series of scenes run without a Cut To, they end at the next Cut To. You always end a series of scenes with a Cut To.

TRANSITIONS YOU SHOULDN'T USE

Other than the four transitions, there are many more which are sometimes offered. For the most part they are not screenwriting terms but editing or cinematography terms. We try to not use these, just as we avoid directing and camera terms unless essential to the story. Some of these include:

DISSOLVE, CROSSFADE, or LAP DISSOLVE: When one scene fades out as the next fades in under it. Like a dissolve, it melds the two scenes together but there is a moment of black between them.

FADE: The scene fades while the next scene is fully present. It seems like a dissolve.

JUMP CUT: The editing jumps to an angle breaking continuity, jarring the audience.

L CUT or J CUT: An audio cut which laps the audio into the next scene (L) or starts the next scene's audio before the scene cuts (J).

MATCH or FORM CUT and MATCH DISSOLVE: Often designed by cinematographers so that the focus and/or shapes of one scene matches the point of focus or shapes in the next scene.

CONTRAST CUT: A juxtaposition of disparate images.

SMASH or STRAIGHT CUT: An abrupt transition often used to show destruction, violence, or rapid changes of emotion.

TIME CUT: Advancing forward in a scene to pass over the mundane elements of time. This is the MOMENT LATER type of cut.

WIPE: The retro look of the next scene sliding across the current scene, wiping it out.

In each case, it is the decision of the director, cinematographer, and editor as to which of these will be used. And the screenwriter should not be worrying about this stage of filmmaking since it is not relevant to writing a great screenplay.

CHAPTER 11
DIALOGUE BLOCKS

Character Cue - Vocal Origination - Off Screen - Off Camera - Telephone Voice - Voice-Over - Translated Dialogue - Parentheticals or Personal and Vocal Direction - Dialogue - Dialogue Timing - Numbers - Abbreviations - Acronyms - the Ellipsis in Dialogue - the Em Dash in Dialogue - Dialogue Page Breaks - Dialogue Continues Across Action - Dialogue Interruptions

D ialogue is the most important part of any screenplay, because that is what the audience will experience most about the script. When the motion picture is finished, the descriptions disappear, the format disappears, but the dialogue, the artfulness of screenwriter's actual words, remain.

The craft of a Dialogue Block is much easier. The Dialogue Block is designed to be easily read and stand out from the description of the script. In this way is easy for the actors to concentrate only on the dialogue.

> THE AUTHOR (V.O.)
> The block consists of the
> Character Cue naming the
> speaker, the Vocal Origination
> explaining where the voice is
> coming from if needed, the
> Dialogue, and
> (pausing for effect)
> Parentheticals which can give
> vocal or action direction for
> the actor while speaking.

CHARACTER CUE

Each dialogue block begins with a cue for the actor using the actor's character name written in capitals. The Character Cue (sometimes called a character slug) is indented three tabs from the left margin. It is sometimes followed by a vocal origination or a continued, if they are warranted.

DAVE

Obviously, the choice of a character's name is important in projecting their personality. For the character cue, use the most common use of their name. If you have a character named Dave Wilson and refer to him in description as Dave, don't use the character cue WILSON or DAVE WILSON. Call him DAVE.

Use distinct names for characters. It is confusing to have JOHN, JON, and JOE speaking to each other. Be clear about who smaller characters are and use unique titles or names for each different character. Don't call all policemen COP. It's confusing. Use COP 1 and JUDITH THE WAITRESS.

It is important to always use the same name for any character. Do not introduce the Mysterious Stranger and later give him the name Dave. Introduce him as "a Mysterious Stranger who will come to known as Dave" and use Dave as the character cue. Switching names confuses the reader, the production company, and the actor. Readers are not the audience so you do not need to keep mysterious things from them. In this case, they may not know who Dave is but the warning makes it clearer when reading the screenplay. And you want to be clear.

VOCAL ORIGINATION

Vocal Origination is used to indicate where the voice of a character comes from if they are not seen on camera.

OFF SCREEN

Off Screen indicates that the character is speaking from a different Set, such as the next room or calling from outside.

                    BERNIE (O.S.)
        Are you in there, Mona?

OFF CAMERA

More an effect term, Off Camera is used when a character is in the room but not seen on camera; when you want to surprise the character on screen with a voice of someone who is unexpected.

                    BERNIE (O.C.)
        Guess who!

FILTERED VOICE

When a character is heard over a radio, a telephone, a walkie talkie, TV, recording, etc., they are said to be "filtered." Unlike a Voice Over, which is not heard by the characters in a scene, the Filtered Voice is heard by characters. Another Filtered Voice might be the disembodied voice of God or the voice of a ghost or spirit talking to a character. Filtered is an indicator to production team that the actor need not be on set and that the voice can be recorded separately from the scene.

                    BERNIE (FILTERED)
        Honey, I won't be home 'til
        seven. We had a meeting. I'll
        pick up Chinese takeout.

VOICE-OVER

When a character or narrator is speaking over the scene and unheard by the characters within the scene, narrating events or speaking from an inner voice (a character's thoughts), use (V.O.). This means the person speaking is not in the scene at all or the person in the scene is not speaking but thinking or narrating. Even when the character is NARRATOR you use (V.O.).

                    BERNIE (V.O.)
          I thought I was smarter than
          that but here I was making the
          same mistake all over again.

TRANSLATED DIALOGUE

Often in a film you will have characters who speak in a foreign language. Sometimes you do not want this translated when your other characters are not supposed to understand what the speaker is saying. In this case you can use the foreign dialogue:

> GENERAL FRANCO
> Soy responsable solamente a dios
> y a la historia.

This tells the actor to say it in the foreign language and to not translate it for the audience. But it is better to translate the line and use the Vocal Origination (TRANSLATED). This lets the reader understand the story but still indicates that the production will translate the line for the actor and not to subtitle it.

> GENERAL FRANCO (TRANSLATED)
> I am responsible only to God and
> history

If you want the actor to speak in a foreign language and have subtitles on the screen to translate for the audience, you use the Vocal Origination of (SUBTITLED).

> GENERAL FRANCO (SUBTITLED)
> I am responsible only to God and
> history

Using the Translated and Subtitled Vocal Originations also means that the reader knows what is being said for purposes of reading. Don't include both the foreign language and the translation in the script since it throws off the reader and fails to present the proper format timing.

PARENTHETICALS OR PERSONAL AND VOCAL DIRECTION

Often below the character cue comes the Parenthetical, which can either be Personal Direction or Vocal Direction. Parentheticals allow you to suggest the way a speaker says a line (vocal) or do some physical action (personal) without having to break the speech with scene description. Parentheticals are inset two tabs from the left margin, surrounded by brackets (parentheses), and should not exceed three words. This positioning assures that the reader or actor will not accidentally read them as dialogue.

Example (Four parentheticals - (1) vocal, (2) personal, (3) vocal, and (4) personal.)

```
              LORD HARRY
            (nervously)
      I'll fight you but this is
      better settled in court.
            (to his Second)
      I choose the pearl handled
      pistol.
            (pause)
      Thank you.
            (cocking pistol)
      I'm ready.
```

Notice how you can imply action here. The (pause) is the time it will take for the Second to hand Lord Harry his pistol. When he thanks his Second we know he has it. And you didn't have to describe the action at all. But it's definitely implied.

Parentheticals are only for the character speaking and only relate to the way in which the dialogue is given: such as personal action (into phone) or personal emotion (terrified).

Try to avoid using vocal direction to suggest emotions. Most vocal direction is implied in your dialogue anyway. If you tell the actor they should be terrified and they are yelling, "Please, don't kill me" it is rather redundant. It can, sometimes, be insulting to an actor who may think you don't believe actors can read a script and understand the emotions required. But there are cases where you will find it important to include vocal directions.

One of the most common parentheticals is (pause), which indicates that the speaker breaks their dialogue for a moment either to think about something or what to say next, to pause for emphasis, or wait for something to be done. You should not use the word "beat" since that is an acting and directing term. And only use a pause if it not naturally indicated in the dialogue itself. Pauses are often natural in speech and punctuation. Words like "Well, " indicate a slight pause as does a comma or an ellipsis. If someone is on the phone and they say, "Yes, I understand" it means they have paused to listen and no (pause) is needed. Actors are trained to do this and can be insulted by the overuse of writer's pauses.

Personal direction parentheticals are useful when it is important for the speaker to turn or speak directly to another actor or into a phone, since it has to do with how the dialogue works. It can only relate directly to that speaker and no other character. It also must be something which effects the character's act of speaking. If it is anything more it should be put out at the margin as description.

Parentheticals are very useful, but, when overused, like breaking up dialogue with action, can cause the scene or dialogue to sound choppy and lose its impact for the reader.

DIALOGUE

The Dialogue itself is left and right indented. It runs from the first tab in from the left margin to the start of the last tab on the right. The dialogue therefore runs 3.5 inches wide (or 35 characters). Some word processors do this by indenting the margins during dialogue. Dialogue is where the screenwriter must excel. Dialogue is the heart of the screenplay.

Dialogue, like action, does not have automatic hyphenation at the end of line and is left justified only. This makes it easier to scan, read, or speak.

Example. (Dialogue)

```
                ROMEO
   Hark, what light through yonder
   window breaks.  It is the moon,
   and Juliet is the sun.
```

DIALOGUE TIMING

In dialogue it is important to be clear in your spelling and punctuation. Since an actor has to speak these words, you want to be exact in your writing to not confuse him or her.

```
                    DAVE
      I think it was his ID.  He
      worked for the CIA.  I know that
      his IQ was 185.  Oddly, he lived
      at 185 Bolt Ave.  I think he
      lived with Ms. Thomas.  Yes.  Or
      is it Mrs. Thomas?
```

This piece of dialogue contains a number of problems. First, Standard Format should match the time it takes to say a piece of dialogue. This dialogue block doesn't run at the time it would take to say it because so many of the abbreviations, numbers, and acronyms are condensed. Let's break it down:

NUMBERS

Do you want the actor to say "one hundred eighty five" or "a hundred and eight five" or "one eight five." They are all different ways of saying 185. This become even harder with longer numbers. It is important to write them out the way you want them to be spoken.

ABBREVIATIONS

Most abbreviations are longer when spoken so it is wise to type them out. Dr. should be Doctor, esq. is Esquire, and HRM is Her Royal Majesty or H.R.M. While most readers and actors accept Mr., Mrs, and Ms. as abbreviations, you are always better off writing out Mister, Missus, and Miz. In the case of Ave, should the actor say "Ave" or "Avenue"? Again this adds clarity for the actor and accurate timing for the filmmakers.

ACRONYMS

Is it I.D. or id with emphasis? If it is the acronym I.D., meaning Identification, then you need the periods, or full stops, meaning making a full stop after each letter. This is also true of CIA which is actually C.I.A. If you mean id with emphasis you would write id and underline it (id). Some acronyms are pronounced as words like ASCAP or FEMA, requiring no periods. Most are a series of letters like F.B.I. Some are more complex like NAACP, which would be, in dialogue, N. Double A.C.P. Sound the acronym out and write it as it should be spoken by the actor.

QUOTES

If your character is quoting or reading from another work such as a letter or from literature or a quote, poem, or song lyrics, use quote marks (" ") to set the quote off. Actors know how to deal with this when they perform. Also, when quoting poetry, don't cut the lines the way the poet did but use slash marks (/).

```
                TOM
    Here is it. "And all my life
    until this day, / And all my
    life until I die, / All joy
    and sorrow of the way, / Seem
    calling yonder in the sky; /
    And there is something the song
    saith / That makes me unafraid
    of death."
```

THE ELLIPSIS IN DIALOGUE

Ellipsis (plural ellipses; from the Ancient Greek: lleipsis, "omission" or "falling short") is a series of marks that usually indicate an intentional omission of a word in the original text. An ellipsis can also be used to indicate a pause in speech, an unfinished thought, or, at the end of a sentence, a trailing off into silence (aposiopesis). When placed at the end of a sentence, the ellipsis can also inspire a feeling of melancholy longing. The ellipsis calls for a slight pause in speech.

The most common form of an ellipsis is a row of three periods or full stops (...) or a pre-composed triple-dot glyph (…). The usage of the em dash (—) can overlap the usage of the ellipsis.

The triple-dot punctuation mark is also called a suspension point, points of ellipsis, periods of ellipsis, or colloquially, dot-dot-dot.

They are most useful in dialogue to show the loss of thought, a pause to think, or stuttering.

```
                  TOM
   I think I...  Well, I...  Yes,
   I think I was in the house at
   the time.  But I was pa... pu..
   powerful scared.
```

When using an ellipsis always leave a space after the ellipses and before the next word. While you shouldn't overuse this contrivance, it can also help you avoid parenthetical pauses.

THE EM DASH IN DIALOGUE

Most people know how to use the hyphen. Screenwriters use them in Scene Headings to set off the Time of Day. Hyphens also link two words into a composite word such as self-help or ex-husband.

But the Em Dash is important to screenwriters since it does effect how dialogue is spoken. The em dash is a double hyphen (the same width as an "m"). In a sentence, it has no spaces on either side of it. It is like an aside in a sentence. Since you can't use brackets () in dialogue which might be mistaken for a parenthetical, you use an em dash. There are three uses in dialogue:

1. To set off parenthetical material for emphasis: "I don't have any idea how—from the arrival of your mother to the departure of our son—you can blame me."

2. To set off appositives, such as a list in the middle of a sentence that has commas, so as to differentiate the commas: "Tom had thought of everything—tent, gear, food, etcetera—that they would need for the trip."

3. To set up an amplification, restatement, or dramatic shift in tone or thought: "They were guided by a higher power—a godly, heavenly power—that they could not ignore" or "You haven't answered—are you listening—why you were late to school."

The em dash should not be overused. It does not end sentences and should not be used when a comma, colon, semi-colon, or ellipsis will do.

While many word processors create em dashes by pressing Shift, Alt, and hyphen together, check your software for its own shortcut to create em dashes.

DIALOGUE PAGE BREAKS

While scene description never breaks across a page break, there are times when dialogue is long and must continue onto the next page.

Most screenwriting software automatically breaks dialogue at the end of the closest convenient end of sentence, adds a parenthetical (MORE), and puts the next sentence on the next page, repeating the Character Cue with the Vocal Origination of (CONT'D).

Example:

```
            LORD HARRY
We have suffered many losses
and many of our comrades have
suffered wounds which prevent
them from continuing with us.
But we must go forward in the
battle and win the day.
            (MORE)
```

page break

```
                              12


            LORD HARRY (CONT'D)
And we must find the means to
persevere in the face of greater
odds than we have ever faced in
this glorious campaign.
```

If you are not using screenwriting software, and the dialogue gets to the bottom of a page and the page will only hold the Character Cue, move the whole dialogue block to the next page. If the dialogue is long enough to have multiple sentences and would break across a page, break the dialogue after a sentence end. Put a parenthetical (MORE) after the break of the dialogue and make a new dialogue block on the next page. The Character

Cue is followed on the second page with a vocal origination of (CONT'D). This will enable the reader to read each page to a complete sentence. Also, the actor performing the role will not break a sentence, pausing to turn the page.

DIALOGUE CONTINUES ACROSS ACTION

The same vocal origination (CONT'D), as in dialogue page breaks, can be used when dialogue on a page is broken by an action which happens at the same time as the dialogue. For instance a character is giving a speech and someone enters the hall during the speech.

>   LORD HARRY
>   We must go forward in the battle
>   and win the day.
>
> As Harry speaks the rival army arrives on
> the edge of hill behind him.
>
>   LORD HARRY (CONT'D)
>   And we must find the means to
>   persevere in the face of greater
>   odds than we have ever faced.

If the speaker stops talking for an action to take place and resumes speaking afterwards, this is not a continued situation and you would not use a (CONT'D).

>   JACK
>   Well, that's done!
>
> The tree he's planted slowly falls over. He
> walks to it to see the roots exposed.
>
>   JACK
>   Not my day!

Screenwriting software, unable to decide whether action is interrupting the speaker or not, automatically adds the (CONT'D). You can take control of this by turning the auto option off and properly judging whether or not to use the (CONT'D). It is not considered a real problem if you let the software do this, but it is always better to have full control over your screenplay.

DUAL DIALOGUE

In cases where two people are speaking at the same time, the screenwriter should separate the voices and run them side by side as dual dialogue with two character cues.

Example of the wrong way to do it.

```
                    TOM AND JERRY
         We agree!
```

In the example above, the problem for the production is that there is no character named TOM AND JERRY. There are two characters and their voices must be distinct. Dual Dialogue division covers this. In screenwriting software this is accomplished by a convenient short cut built into the system. In regular word processors this can be done with tabs, dual columns, or by setting up a table with two columns. So it should look like this:

```
      TOM                      JERRY
We both agree!          We agree!

              TOM
     We met earlier and discussed it.
```

WHY? This serves a couple of purposes. Mainly it tells each of the actors to mark their script for their line and to attempt to say the line at the same time as the other actor. When the breakdown software reads a script it seeks out elements which are inset by tabs and records any that are capitalized. It assumes these are Character Cues and records the character in the database. If you don't do dual dialogue, the production will have a character named "TOM AND JERRY." You can see how confusing this can be. If Jerry's only line in this scene were "We agree" the production might miss listing him since his character cue is buried in Tom's.

DIALOGUE INTERRUPTIONS

In literature when one character interrupts another, the dialogue of the first cuts off, often using an ellipsis. This works because our mind allows the dominant voice - the interrupter - to overpower and drown out the original speaker. But in film, this doesn't happen. This is because of the realities of filming real actors saying real lines and hearing exactly what happens when one person interrupts another. In fact, when one person interrupts another, the first speaker does not immediately stop speaking. The dialogue overlaps.

When production deals with interrupted dialogue, the actor begins his/her dialogue and reacts naturally to the interrupter. Sometimes this means they stop talking when the other's dialogue registers, or he/she peters off the dialogue, or they finish their dialogue falling off in volume. They need the full dialogue to be able to choose what moment works best for their character.

I've been on set when one of these script problems came up. The writer had cut off the dialogue before the logic of the sentence became clear. The actor didn't know how to continue the line and it wasn't enough for the other actor to cut him off without screaming. It was something like...

                    TOM
        I know I was around somewhere.
        It was dark and Molly was
        crying. I think...

                    DETECTIVE WINSTON
                    (interrupting)
        You're saying you can't
        distinguish one landmark that
        might tell us where you were?

The actor playing Tom had no idea what the character would have said after "I think" and the actor playing Detective Winston needed the moment after Molly was mentioned to build up his anger to interrupt. The director cursed the writer, who was not on set, and asked for suggestions on what might be a good line for the actor which could be cut off by the second actor. Some grip came up with a suggestion which seemed to work for the actor playing Tom and the scene was completed.

Ultimately, in writing a screenplay, unlike other literary forms, the interruption is not about stopping the speaker's line but warning the second actor that he or she will be interrupting. The first actor should not anticipate being interrupted. So, you need to complete the first line and parenthetically tell the second actor to break into it wherever makes sense. The secret is that the first character should have his full thought written out because he shouldn't know the second character is going to interrupt him. The writer is telling the second actor to cut in at the appropriate time.

```
               TOM
  I know I was around somewhere.
  It was dark and Molly was
  crying.  I think I was so
  distracted by her crying I
  wasn't paying attention.


           DETECTIVE WINSTON
             (interrupting)
  You're saying you can't
  distinguish one landmark that
  might tell us where you were?
```

The actor playing the detective and the director will make sure that Tom is interrupted somewhere during Tom's last line.

CHAPTER 12
SCENE DESCRIPTION

Spacing - Capitalization - New Character Introductions - Sounds - Brevity - Active Description - Camera Direction - Establishing Shots and Stock Footage - Montage and Shot / Scene Series - Montage - Shot Series - Scene Series - Description Terms You May Not Want to Use - P.O.V. Or Point of View - Angle on and Another Angle - Back to Scene

S cene Description sets up what the characters are doing physically, and how they interact with each other and their physical surroundings. Because the reader is trying to visualize the film the writer is imagining, scene description should be lucid without being too detailed. Too many details tend to slow the reader, breaking the fluidity of the imagination. Mood and action are the elements which most inspire the imagination of a reader.

```
Malcolm stumbles forward through the light
fog toward the looming Gothic church at the
end of the street.  On either side, barely
lit by occasional streetlamps, are deserted
lots and salvage yards.  Vicious dogs bang
against the steel fences as he passes.

The grand ballroom glitters in candle
light.  The floor is a swirl of white gowns
and black tuxes.  The music stops suddenly
as the Princess, in a flowing red gown,
steps out onto the balcony.
```

SPACING

The Scene Description should scan easily. This is accomplished by editing the longer passages of description into blocks of not more than four to six lines. Action sequences which often last a page or more should never fill the page. The break of a blank white line every four to six lines makes it easier for the reader to keep his or her place while scanning an action line.

In description, automatic hyphenation and justification are turned off, as it is also turned off in dialogue, making it easier to read.

One of the ways you can use spacing to your advantage is to organize and space lines by how you visualize a scene. You can use blank lines to indicate changes to different shots. For instance, if you want a close-up of a hand picking up a gun, leave a blank line, and set the line apart. This will indicate the moment should be an insert shot without having to use cumbersome production terms.

```
The Detective holds his gun on the Burglar
who sits on the edge of the coffee table by
the briefcase.

The Burglar's hand reaches secretively
behind him.  His fingers stretch to take
hold of the pistol hidden in the briefcase.

The Detective senses the move and walks
around to slam the briefcase closed.
```

Above, the first paragraph is a wide shot and the second paragraph seems like a close-up and is easy to read. If both sentences were in the same paragraph the imagery would not be as vivid. As you get better and better this will become second nature.

Above all else, you want the script to be easy to read, to hold the reader's attention, and to help him or her to visualize the motion picture it should become.

CAPITALIZATION

Capitalized WORDS in Scene Description should be kept to a minimum. This is an area which is dealt with in the Shooting Script. In the Draft Script a lot of capitalization takes away from the reader's fluid enjoyment and visualization of your story.

NEW CHARACTER INTRODUCTIONS

Whenever you introduce a new character to the story you need to capitalize his or her name the first time they appear in the script. This allows the reader to know that we haven't seen this character before. This is only done once with each character and only when they are actually seen or heard, not simply referred to. You should also give a brief description of their appearance or personality which will help the reader visualize the character.

SOUNDS

While some writing gurus say you should capitalize all sounds, you really shouldn't. Sound recordists, editors, and mixers are quite capable of and prefer to highlight elements in a script and make lists of sounds that should also be there.

The rare case where you might want to capitalize a word is when you need IMPACT! You might want to accent the SLAM of the door which makes the character leap in fear. You also might like to capitalize the first time the FOGHORN blares and the shipwrecked lifeboat sailors know they are near another ship. But don't overuse this. Here are some examples of where the capitalizing of sounds might help the reading of your script:

```
Granny rocks in her chair stroking the cat
who softly purrs in her lap. A loud YELP of
the dog startles her as it leaps away from
the rocker to lick its injured tail.
```

or

Lying in their foxhole, Joe and Dave listen to the distant rat-a-tat-tat of machine guns and the occasional boom, boom, boom of shells hitting around the enemy position.

Then, a loud whistling sound. As it grows in intensity, Joe and Dave dig their faces into the soft ground until...

BOOM! A shell lands nearby sending dirt and debris over them, the concussion knocking the breath from their lungs.

In each chase the writer is using the capitals for IMPACT! If the writer chose to capitalize every sound, the reading of these descriptions would be less powerful, less like the effect the writer wants from the film when it is made.

As the shooting script is developed by the film crew, they will collectively add lots of things which belong but were not detailed in the draft script. They may capitalize or highlight elements to help them during production. They will also add elements they think might enhance the naturalism of the scene. Because you are keeping your description to a minimum, you don't want to do all the filmmaker's work or limit their creative enhancement of your story. Once you say a "meadow at dusk" or "the African veldt," leave it to them to add the detail of crickets chirring and bats whizzing or lions roaring and hyenas laughing.

BREVITY

The big challenge in writing scene description is to keep it simple, to use a style which creates a visual image in your reader's mind without slowing down the reading experience. The convention of a novel allows the writer to spend a great deal of time describing the inner thoughts of characters and their view of events. This is not accepted in the screenplay. In film, the inner journey of the characters is made evident through their action.

You want to set the scene quickly with a brief description of the important elements of the surroundings and introduce the characters involved. Then the action moves through the events of the scene. Only the essential visual elements are mentioned, things which will be employed by the characters. How and when characters move and where tells us about their character, they do things which reveal who they are.

There is not time, in description, for asides or writer's cute phrases. They detract from the power of the story.

ACTIVE DESCRIPTION

It is important to keep the pace of the script moving forward. One way to accomplish this is to use the simple present verb tense. It's easy. Find and remove "is" or "are" before verbs. These are present progressive verb forms. If you have written, for example:

```
Tom is moving around behind the burglar.
```

change it to the simple present:

```
Tom moves around behind the burglar.
```

Writing in the simple present quickens the read by requiring fewer words, often saving pages over the course of a screenplay. It makes the story more exciting, because you reinforce the idea of being in the immediate present, that exact visual moment.

CAMERA DIRECTION

Some readers take offense at having to read the words "WE SEE" or "THE CAMERA DOLLIES IN ON." When reading a script, the reader and the filmmakers want to be there in the story. They want to see what the audience would see at the theater, not what the crew and the extras see making a movie.

Here is a Scene Description with excessive shooting detail:

```
INT. DETECTIVE'S OFFICE - NIGHT

The CAMERA is CLOSE UP on the back of a
door with the name "Spam Sade, Private
Investigator" backwards on the glass.

INSERT: CLOSE UP of the hand of the
detective pulling a bottle of Gorgon's Gin
from the top right drawer of the desk.

BACK TO SCENE

The CAMERA PULLS BACK to reveal SPAM SADE,
a gritty faced private detective in his
late forties, as he pours himself a glass
of gin.  He sits back, stretching his
pained back, and slugs down a shot of the
gin. He looks up and around.  The CAMERA
PANS across the sordid office, coming to
rest on a MEDIUM SHOT of the door.  There
is the CLICK, CLICK of high heels in
the hall as a shadow rises on it, the
silhouette of tall, slim woman in a broad
veiled hat.  The shadow seems reluctant to
enter, then forces the door open.  The door
opens revealing the sultry, thirtyish SHARY
MAUNESSEY.  We don't see her face until
the door opens enough to let the desk lamp
light it.
```

That does describe the scene and makes certain that the filmmakers know what you think they should do with it. But then you might have written it this way:

```
INT. DETECTIVE'S OFFICE - NIGHT

The light in the outer hall backlights the
reversed name on the office door glass:
"Spam Sade, Private Investigator."

A man's hand pulls open the desk drawer and
removes a half empty bottle of gin.

SPAM SADE, gritty, late forties, pours
himself a glass, leans back, trying to ease
the pain in his back, and slugs down the
gin.

He surveys his sordid office, stopping his
gaze on the door as he hears the sound of
high heels approaching.

The silhouette of a slim woman in a veiled
hat rises on the glass as she approaches.
After a hesitation, SHARY MAUNESSEY,
blonde, stunning and twenty-five, opens the
door, her face slowly revealed to the light
of the desk lamp.
```

They both say the exactly same thing. One is a dictatorial explanation of how to shoot a scene. The other is a seductive image which will end up being shot exactly the way it's written and probably with the exact camera movement and cutting as the first version. And is less words. Which would you rather read? Which would provoke you to say, "Now, that would make a great scene." Which makes you imagine it?

A trick is to cut paragraphs when you want the camera to cut. This can be a problem if you want all the action in one shot but you can work out your own language for that.

Many of the Hollywood scripts you read are written with camera direction. Remember, most of these scripts are Final Scripts written after the film is completed, often based on the shooting script and not on the screenwriter's draft script. Much of the description is there to help international editors with dubbing foreign language versions of the film.

An example of the Shooting Script is the INSERT. A draft script never uses this term. It is usually a cue for a non-dialogue element which needs to be subtitled or reshot and inserted with the correct foreign language.

```
The newsboy runs down the street waving a
special edition of the Times.

INSERT; The newspaper headline reads "WAR
DECLARED WITH SAMOA!"

BACK TO SCENE
```

A screenwriter would never do that. The use of the INSERT with BACK TO SCENE is not a screenwriting convention. But it may be important for the Final Script. It means that the headline should be translated into whatever language the film is being dubbed into. In some cases the production supplies textless versions of close-ups so that foreign languages can be optically inserted. But a draft screenplay should not include this type of technical intrusion into the reading nor waste that much precious space on a close-up.

```
The newsboy runs down the street waving a
special edition of the Times.

The newspaper headline reads "WAR DECLARED
WITH SAMOA!"

The Prince reaches for a copy and pays the
boy.
```

ESTABLISHING SHOTS AND STOCK FOOTAGE

The Establishing Shot is a short scene without major characters which introduces the audience to a location, usually when the next scene does not automatically explain the location. The establishing shot is a low-budget way of avoiding shooting exteriors of a location which would require a company move or additional shoot days for lead actors. Ideally, the screenwriter prefers to think that every scene will be shot for the film and writes scenes with the main characters entering a location or develops a montage or shot series which brings the audience into a major new location.

Just as the choice to use an establishing shot, the use of Stock Footage is a choice made by the production. The screenwriter assumes that the scene will be re-created for the film. But when this is too expensive or complicated, the production may decide to purchase stock footage or create footage through computer generated graphics (CGI).

If the screenwriter decides either is essential to the script, the information can be put in the scene heading as set information surrounded with parentheses.

```
EXT. CITY HALL, (ESTABLISHING SHOT) - DAY
```

or

```
INT. POLITICAL RALLY, (STOCK FOOTAGE) - DAY
```

MONTAGE AND SHOT / SCENE SERIES

Montage and Shot Series are often confused. Montage is a simple means to advance time in a story and the Shot Series is a way to progress time quickly while continuing to develop story.

MONTAGE

The montage is a means to condense space, time, and information without exhaustively explaining all the events between majors scenes. The basic premise of the montage (from Fr. montage "a mounting," from O.Fr. monter "to go up, mount") is that a series of quick images which, when juxtaposed, give a sense of the time which is passing before the next major scene takes place. A montage can be as simple as the exterior of a train with steam billowing from the stacks and the pistons churning the wheels down the track. This would take us from one place to another. Another familiar montage is the hands of a clock advancing to show how many hours have passed.

The montage does not include major characters from the script. It is often shot by a secondary unit of the film crew and does not involve the primary director of the film. If it involved the main character or needs the primary director it becomes a shot series. Montages do not contain dialogue (though they may have a V.O.) and are often used as musical interludes.

Here is a familiar montage. When possible, it is advisable to use the traditional scene heading format. To define it as a montage use (MONTAGE) at the end of the Location Set portion of the heading.

```
INT. DOCTOR'S OFFICE, (MONTAGE) - DAY

The pages of the calendar blow away from
July to December.  The December page has a
large red circle around the 15th.

                                    CUT TO:
```

The more complex montage is a series of individual scenes which briefly show a series of events which happen but do not need detail and advance the story forward in time or space. Once the montage requires more than a simple paragraph to explain it, it has a Scene Heading, a description of the purpose of the montage, and a list of elements required to make the montage effective.

The individual elements are given letters which will aid the production. Since the overall scene gets a scene number, the letters indicate each of the elements as a separate shot, just the way a production labels shots on the camera slate: scene 12 - shot A - take 1, etc.

```
EXT. MINNESOTA FARM, FIELDS (MONTAGE) - DAY

The seasons pass from spring to winter.

  A) Farmers plow the fields

  B) Workers sow seed down the earth rows.

  C) Workers check the buds as they sprout.

  D) Workers climb into harvesters and
harvest the crop.

  E) The empty fields lie fallow as the
snow begins to fall.

                              CUT TO:
```

The use of transition CUT TO ends a montage.

The Russian montage theory of Sergei Eisenstein is a different subject having to do with directing and editing.

SHOT SERIES

Similar but more complex than a montage is a Shot Series (sometimes called a Shot Series). It is not actually a montage. It progresses story and not just time. It can be used for character development showing a character improving or changing

Like the montage, the shot series does not have dialogue, though it can have a voice over. The moment dialogue enters a scene, it is not shot series but a separate scene.

```
INT. CHINATOWN DOJO, (SHOT SERIES) - DAY

Ming Wa trains for the big fight.

    A)  Ming Wa moves awkwardly at the
Teacher and is easily thrown to the ground.

    B) Ming Wa watches the Teacher
demonstrate the moves in slow motion with
another student.

    C) Ming Wa moves quickly forward and
throws the Teacher down.  She bows and a
big grin appears on her face.

                            CUT TO:
```

As you can see it is less interesting to read because of the technical element of the bullet letters. But it indicates that the scene probably takes place over a longer period of time than a single scene would.

For a more complex series which covers a number of locations, you can use the modified scene heading without the Time of Day If it has a number of settings you can use I/E showing it has both interiors and exteriors. If elements are various day and night shots, indicate the time of day in the element. and leave the time of day in the heading blank and give each element a time of day.

```
INT/EXT. CHINATOWN DOJO, (SHOT SERIES) -

Ming Wa trains for the big fight.
```

A) Ming Wa moves awkwardly at Teacher and is easily thrown to the ground - DAY

B) Ming Wa leaves on her bicycle in great pain - NIGHT

C) Ming Wa watches Teacher demonstrate the moves in slow motion with another student - DAY

D) Ming Wa arrives refreshed at dojo - DAY

E) Ming Wa moves quickly forward and throws the Teacher down. She bows and a big grin appears on her face - DAY

SCENE SERIES

A Scene Series is short scenes which progress the story. It's not really different from doing individual scene but is distinctive with its lack of transitions. It can contain dialogue. You don't need to indicate it is a scene series but if there is room, you can insert (SCENE SERIES) in the first heading.

INT. KREMLIN, OFFICE (SCENE SERIES) - DAY

The Chairman shakes his head and grabs the phone.

INT. WHITE HOUSE, BEDROOM - NIGHT

The President rouses from sleep as the phone rings. He listens and stands, angry.

INT. JAPANESE MINISTRY, LARGE HALL - DAY

The Japanese Minister of Defense paces.

                              CUT TO:

DESCRIPTION TERMS YOU SHOULD NOT USE

Like the term INSERT, there are a lot of words which should be avoided. They cause a number of problems: 1) they are not very descriptive, 2) they waste a lot of lines, 3) in screenplay format they may be mistaken for scene headings since they are capitalized, and, finally, 4) they conflict with storytelling and are annoying for the people who make screenplays into motion pictures.

Overall, any description which is capitalized is suspect screenwriting language and should be avoided.

P.O.V. or POINT OF VIEW

Often, a shot from the character's point of view is an important aspect to the storytelling. While you can use the term P.O.V., it is easier to use terms such as the character "watches" or the character "sees" which means that what is seen is a point of view shot. While the term P.O.V. isn't that offensive to the reader and crew, it is better to get into using "John spies on the intruders," "Tina sees her husband hide the package," or "Detective Norman watches the couple from across the street, through the trees." Each of these would be a P.O.V. shot.

ANGLE ON and ANOTHER ANGLE

A camera instruction about placing the camera in another no-no. Why is the screenwriter suggesting this? The screenwriter is not the one to choose the camera angles.

BACK TO SCENE

Back To Scene is not description or action, it is a scene heading meaning that the previous material was a different scene. If that is true, use the full scene heading instead of this nebulous instruction. If you mean cut back to scene from a specific shot in that scene, don't use this term at all.

CHAPTER 13
PUNCTUATION, GRAMMAR, & SPELLING

O ne of the worst things a screenwriter can do to a reader is to submit a screenplay with poor punctuation, incorrect grammar, and spelling mistakes. Character is developed in a screenplay through the use of action and dialogue. Dialogue is only clear when it is properly punctuated. It may sound like a small thing, but the misuse of the comma is annoying and seems as unprofessional to a reader, or an actor, as poorly constructed description or the use of filmmaking terms.

There is a rumor that actors don't like the writer to punctuate the dialogue or to add necessary parenthetical directions. This is not true for most actors. The few who do ask that punctuation and parentheticals be removed are probably spoiled, enjoy torturing production assistants (who will have to do the editing), and don't really care what the screenwriter was thinking when he or she wrote the script. Don't worry about them. Professional actors appreciate the writer's ability to enhance the qualities of their character. Ignore this rumor and write correctly and professionally.

```
                MARY
   Is that a hair Bob?  Well Bob, I
   think you should consider a lint
   brush.  Oh my god I have one in
   my bag.  Would you use it if I
   lent it to you do you think?
```

It seems simple, but remember that a comma is a slight pause in speech. If Mary is referring to a hair style it is only a typo. If she is talking to a character named Bob, it is funny. And the last line seems to make no sense. How simple it would be to write:

```
              MARY
Is that a hair, Bob? Well, Bob,
I think you should consider a
lint brush.  Oh, my god, I have
one in my bag.  Would you use
it if I lent it to you, do you
think?
```

Other examples might be:

```
Bye Missus Winston.
Bye, Missus Winston.
Forget that man!
Forget that, man!
Well come in.
Well, come in.
```

Without the comma after Bye this would be spoken like "Buy Missus Winston." The comma gives the inflection after Bye that separates it from the name. "Forget that man" is completely different from the same sentence with a comma. And the inflection of "Well, come in" is ruined without the comma.

Proper use of the comma sounds like a small thing. But failure to do it can be good for a laugh and a break from reading your script for another cup of coffee. It can be the difference between the writer getting the rewrite or losing it to a more professional screenwriter. Most people can learn the proper use of commas, question marks, colons and semicolons, and exclamation points in a matter of a half hour if they have a copy of that very short book, Strunk and White's "Elements of Style." It's worth the time.

Edit your work and have it proofed by someone else. A screenwriter is supposed to be someone educated in grammar and spelling as much as being able to use the language properly. A script which is badly written and full of grammar and spelling mistakes is not going to be taken seriously. Even if it is a great story, any buyer will immediately consider bringing in a professional who can spell and punctuate properly to rewrite it.

CHAPTER 14
PRESENTATION AND COPYRIGHT

Paper - Presentation Page - Copyright Notices - Copyright Registration - Other Evidentiary Registrations

T he script is usually presented to the reader three-hole punched and may, if you wish, have a hard stock cover and back. The script is bound with two brass brads in the upper and lower punch holes (and brass washers on the back). The presentation (or title) page is the first standard page behind the cover stock. The cover stock can have only the title or the same information as the presentation page of the script. Some literary agencies have their own logo cover stock. You can also use a clear acetate cover so the reader can see through the cover to the presentation page. Another thing you can do is to write the title of your script (and only the title) with black marker along the spine of the bound script making it easy to see when piled or shelved.

PAPER

The page the reader should see should be clean white (not yellow, blue, grey, or straw). Bright white paper is the only paper a script appears on, making seem fresh and new. When your script is printed you want it to feel solid with firm pages but not too thick or too heavy. The standard paper is 22-24 pound (lb.) paper. If you have a longer script (110-120 pages) you might want to use a lighter paper such as 20 lb. Remember, a very heavy feeling script will make the reader think it is a heavy and overlong story.

PRESENTATION PAGE

The presentation (or title) page itself should be simple. The title appears centered one third of the way down the page. It can be in a larger font if you wish, and bold, and can be underlined. Three or four lines down the author(s) name appears centered. If it is based on another work the "based on" information is below the author.

At the right bottom of the page should be the name of the person submitting the script, the contact address, phone number and email. There are only three choices for who submits: the author, the agent for the author who may have a talent agency or entertainment law company name, or the third party producer or production company who has purchased the rights to the script.

Authors should not invent a production company name for themselves. Scripts with production company names on the cover are often thought to be owned by a production company, which means they are not for sale and only looking for financing or distribution.

Do not include a cast of characters ("dramatis personæ") after the presentation page and or include an introduction with production notes or a synopsis. Any information about the script you might wish to add belongs in a cover letter.

This is the way to present a screenplay. Nothing else. No dates, revision numbers, draft numbers, etc. Simple and to the point. If they have any questions they will write, call or email you.

And as for a copyright notice...

COPYRIGHT NOTICES

Current trends suggest you do not put a copyright notice on your screenplay. Technically, the copyright law says that it is not essential and that it is always implied that the work is copyrighted even without a notice. So, let's say you don't put the notice on the script, are you protected and should you officially register it?

COPYRIGHT REGISTRATION

While I won't attempt to advise you on the legalities of copyright law, I will suggest that you would be wise to read the information about registration on the U.S. Copyright Office website (www. copyright.gov/) and confer with an intellectual property or entertainment lawyer about what you should do. Copyright is important for a writer and an integral part of your craft and career. To view it simply, let me quote the FAQ on the Library of Congress Registrar of Copyrights website:

Q: Do I have to register with your office to be protected?
A: No. In general, registration is voluntary. Copyright exists from the moment the work is created. You will have to register, however, if you wish to bring a lawsuit for infringement of a U.S. work. See Circular 1, Copyright Basics, section "Copyright Registration."

There is no reason not to register your work. It is actually expected that you protect your work if you want to sell it, and part of the contract when you sell it. It also protects unsold work. Since copyright protection lasts for your lifetime and seventy years, it is useful since you may wish to pass your work on to your heirs or assigns in the future. Most importantly, the registration makes it easy for someone interested in your work to find you since registration is a public notice which locks in your name, address, and date of birth. This trio of information improves the likelihood that they can find you, even if you have moved or married and changed your name. In the end, it is up to you.

OTHER EVIDENTIARY REGISTRATIONS

Another way to protect your screenplay, for a short period of time, is to register it with the Writers Guild of America. This is not a copyright! It only protects you for five years (ten if you remember to re-register it). The WGA East and WGA West are the screenwriter's union and their registration is designed to be used in arbitration cases, between writers, when two or more work on the same script and have a difference over credit. It can also be used to defend against abuses by producers, production companies, and studios. You should check out their websites for more information on registration. While WGA registration is not a copyright, it can give you temporary protection. The WGA can also register a treatment or outline, something you can't do with the Copyright Office.

But I recommend that you should register your screenplay with the U.S. Copyright Office as a matter of course, simply because it is a part of your life as a professional writer.

CHAPTER 15
THE CHALLENGE

With the rules, comes the challenge. You've got ninety to one hundred and twenty pages to write your story. You've got an idea. And, if you do three pages a day in thirty to forty days you have a screenplay. Just be sure to use proper screenplay format.

While format does not guarantee you success, it will help make your screenplay tighter and will help you write in a manner which will encourage filmmakers to see your work as professional, possible as a film, and easily translated into the visual medium.

Format is just a part of the complex art of screenwriting. But, once mastered, format will free to you to concentrate on the storytelling, the aspect of writing which is unique to the writer. Love what you do, dedicate yourself, and write responsibly.

Good luck and write, write, write.

About the Author

Boston-born Jean-Paul Ouellette pursued filmmaking after completing studies in literature and graphic design when he moved to Los Angeles, apprenticing to filmmakers Russ Meyer and Orson Welles and mentored by television directing legend Don Richardson. Mr. Ouellette worked for such companies as Cannon Pictures, New Line Cinema, Orion Pictures, and Roger Corman's New World Cinema.

He directed the second-unit action sequences for the Hemdale/Orion film "Terminator," directed by James Cameron and starring Arnold Schwarzenegger. He wrote and directed the cult horror films "H.P. Lovecraft's The Unnamable" and its sequel. He has worked as an international television co-producer and produces documentaries, industrials, and indie films. He works as a screenwriter and script consultant. He consults with independent producers; developing projects from concept and script through breakdown, budget, marketing, and funding documentation.

He is on the board of the Woods Hole Film Festival and teaches at Emerson College's professional screenwriting program.

CPSIA information can be obtained
at www.ICGtesting.com
Printed in the USA
FSHW011002230620
71465FS